HI
—
HISTORY

The Untold Stories of

Women During World War I and World War II

By Rachel Basinger

THE UNTOLD STORIES OF WOMEN DURING WORLD WAR I AND WORLD WAR II

1405 SW 6th Avenue • Ocala, Florida 34471 • Phone 352-622-1825 • Fax 352-622-1875
Website: www.atlantic-pub.com • Email: sales@atlantic-pub.com
SAN Number: 268-1250

Library of Congress Cataloging-in-Publication Data

Names: Basinger, Rachel, 1992- author.
Title: Hidden in history : the untold stories of women during WWI and WWII / By Rachel Bostron.
Description: Ocala, Florida : Atlantic Publishing Group, Inc., [2019] | Includes bibliographical references and index.
Identifiers: LCCN 2018039169 (print) | LCCN 2018044122 (ebook) | ISBN 9781620236185 (ebook) | ISBN 9781620236178 (alk. paper) | ISBN 1620236176 (alk. paper)
Subjects: LCSH: World War, 1914-1918—Women. | World War, 1914-1918—Women—Biography. | World War, 1939-1945—Women. | World War, 1939-1945—Women—Biography.
Classification: LCC D639.W7 (ebook) | LCC D639.W7 B66 2019 (print) | DDC 940.3092/52—dc23
LC record available at https://lccn.loc.gov/2018039169

Printed in the United States

PROJECT MANAGER: Danielle Lieneman
COVER DESIGN AND INTERIOR LAYOUT: Nicole Sturk

Over the years, we have adopted a number of dogs from rescues and shelters. First there was Bear and after he passed, Ginger and Scout. Now, we have Kira, another rescue. They have brought immense joy and love not just into our lives, but into the lives of all who met them.

We want you to know a portion of the profits of this book will be donated in Bear, Ginger and Scout's memory to local animal shelters, parks, conservation organizations, and other individuals and nonprofit organizations in need of assistance.

– Douglas & Sherri Brown,
President & Vice-President of Atlantic Publishing

Dedication

To my maternal grandmother, Alice Woomer, for her military service in the 1960s and my paternal grandmother, Harriet Basinger, for her support on the Home Front while my grandfather fought in World War II

Table of Contents

Part I: World War I

Part II: World War II

Chapter 4

Chapter 5

Chapter 6

"I was Short and Embarrassed by it"

Imagine that you're a female Russian underground fighter on the frontlines transporting the wounded. The cry of "Assault!" rings out. As you rush forward, you stumble. Not because you're clumsy. And not because you're ill-qualified to be a soldier. But rather because you're wearing high heels!

Maria Vasilyevna Zhloba was that female Soviet (Russian) soldier moving the wounded out of Minsk when she heard the call of "Assault!" Because she was short and embarrassed by her lack of height, she had been wearing high heels to look taller and fit in with the rest of the men and women.

But her grand plans failed when they had to charge forward. One of Zhloba's heels broke, and she had to run barefoot with the shoes in her hand. Her recollection years later? "A pity, they were beautiful shoes."[1]

---

1. Alexievich, 2017.

Chapter 1

"The Vast Reserve of Woman Power"

As historian John Lukacs notes in "The Legacy of the Second World War", "The two great world wars were the two mountain ranges that dominated the entire history of the twentieth century."[2] Obviously, this is true from the perspective of people involved and killed, technologies developed, country borders changed, and so forth. Another way that World War I and World War II were two mountain ranges that dominated the history of the 20th century is the impact they had on women.

You probably have a vague idea of some of the work women did in World War II, conjuring up an image of a red polka-dotted bandana-clad woman named Rosie the Riveter in your mind. You may also think of the WACs. My maternal grandmother, who would serve in the Army in the 1960s, constantly mentions the spick-and-span uniforms of the WACs and how she would have loved to have been one during World War II. But you probably don't know anything about women in World War I, except maybe vague knowledge about women working as nurses.

---

2. Lukacs, 2010.

In this book, the amazing women who served in a variety of capacities in the World Wars will come to life. You'll meet Maria Bochkareva, a woman who helped to form the Women's Death Battalions in Russia. You'll read about Edith Cavell, a superb spy during World War I whose death caused worldwide indignation. You'll discover Rebecca West, the British dame who covered the Nuremberg War Crimes Trials at the end of World War II. And you'll encounter the sassy Mary Amanda Sabourin, one of the first female Marines and one who stayed in the Corps and retired as a Sergeant Major.

In addition to their incredible stories, you'll also see how the World Wars changed the role of women in society. Because the men went off to war, large numbers of women were recruited to take over their jobs at home, and some women even opted to serve internationally to help the war effort. In the words of American Secretary of War Henry Stimson in 1943, the War Department needed to utilize "the vast reserve of woman power."

For many women, it was their first job outside of the home. After the war ended, some women wanted to keep those jobs — and some did. The vast majority of women went back to the home and remained wonderful homemakers, but the fact that women had completed jobs traditionally reserved for men created a growing awareness for more rights for women. Thus, the World Wars began a slow societal change of gender expectations and roles. And for that reason, you should enjoy studying the "Untold Stories of Women During World War I and World War II."

Part I
World War I

While you may remember less about World War I — then known as The Great War or the World War — than its successor, World War II, the Great War still caused immense devastation throughout Europe and surrounding areas. Comparatively, the mortality rate was almost always higher for World War I in contrast to World War II.[3] Only the Union of Soviet Socialist Russia (USSR)/Russia had higher losses during World War II, in large part due to its ruthless leader Josef Stalin.[4] Unlike World War II, which started almost exclusively because of one man, Adolf Hitler, a variety of nations and individuals contributed to the outbreak of World War I. From Austria-Hungary's original dispute with Serbia to Germany's "blank check" to Britain's willingness to defend Belgium, each European country played a small part in the enlargement of the conflict.

 The "blank check" is a reference to Germany pledging to support Austria-Hungary in defeating Serbia. After the assassination of Archduke Franz Ferdinand, the Austro-Hungarian Foreign Minister drew up a letter for Emperor Franz Josef to sign and send to Germany, Austria's ally, asking for the Kaiser's assistance. On July 6, 1914, the Kaiser and

---

3. Audoin-Rouzeau and Becker, 2002.
4. Ibid.

Imperial Chancellor von Bethmann Hollweg sent a telegram in response, stating "that His Majesty will faithfully stand by Austria-Hungary, as is required by the obligations of his alliance and of his ancient friendship."[5] This telegram became the "blank check" through which Germany assisted Austria in defeating Serbia, no questions asked. In fact, although later deleted before sending the telegram, the original draft stated that the Kaiser would support Austria "under all circumstances."[6] Both Franz Josef and the Kaiser thought that Russia was not prepared to fight and expected the war to be short.

Ever since the Balkan Wars of 1912-1913, conservatives in Austria-Hungary began to fear the rising strength of Serbia and wanted to send a forceful message to it. Their emperor, Franz Josef, was in his 80s, and his heir apparent, Archduke Franz Ferdinand, was holding everything together. Although warned by the Serbian government beforehand of an assassination plot, the Archduke and his wife, Countess Sophie Chotek, decided to proceed with their planned visit to Sarajevo, the capital of Bosnia-Herzegovina, a nation that had sided with the Serbs, on Serbia's National Day: June 28, 1914. The trip was ill-fated: Gavrilo Princip and the Black Hand, an ultranationalist Serbian terrorist group, successfully assassinated the Archduke and his wife, giving Austria-Hungary all the excuse that it needed to punish the Serbs. They issued an ultimatum of 10 stringent demands to Serbia. Surprisingly, Serbia agreed to all except one of the demands, and many countries, including Germany, believed that war had been avoided. Austria-Hungary, however, did not accept the Serbian response and declared war on Serbia on July 28, 1914. Within the next month, almost like a tumbling tower of Jenga blocks, various countries in Europe began to declare war on one another for different reasons until, on August 6, 1914, Great Britain, Russia, Serbia, and France were at war with Austria-Hungary and Germany. As Sir Edward Grey, the British Secretary of State for Foreign Affairs, famously stated, "The lamps are going out all over Europe. We shall not see them lit again in our time."[7]

---

5. Montgelas and Schücking, 1924.

6. Ibid.

7. Persico, 2004.

Country	Reasons for Fighting
Austria-Hungary	Punish Serbia
Germany	Stand by Austria-Hungary
England	Defend Belgian Neutrality
France	Assist Russia & maintain Verdun and Toul
Russia	Stand by Serbia

In an attempt to avoid a two-front war, the Germans utilized the Schlieffen Plan, which required the Germans to go north through Brussels, violating Belgian neutrality, and then south to catch French forces going through Alsace-Lorraine. Confident that the counterclockwise wheeling motion of the plan would act as a giant pincer, the Germans planned to parade in Paris by the end of September 1914. The plan failed. When the French checked the German advance during the First Battle of the Marne (September 5-12, 1914), the "Race to the Sea" began as the French and German armies both attempted to outflank each other west of Paris and gain the upper hand before reaching the English Channel. Neither side prevailed, and the familiar image of World War I — trench warfare — began. The first month of the war also brought about roughly 1 million casualties.

With the brief exception of the Christmas Day Truce on the Western Front in 1914, the next four years on the Western Front would be haunted by the ubiquitous mud of the trenches; the unending gas attacks; the daring of the Flying Aces; the advent of new machines like tanks; the tragedies of frostbite, shellshock, and amputations; and the deaths of millions of European young men and, occasionally, women.

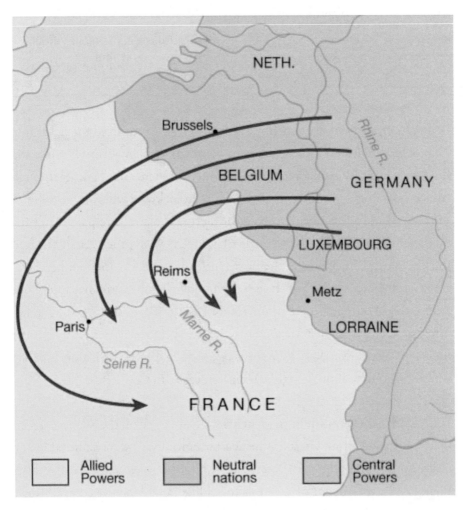

Schlieffen Plan

Famous Battles	Dates of the Battles	Interesting Facts about the Battles
First Battle of Ypres	October 19-November 22, 1914	The British called the First and Second Battles of Ypres "wipers."
Second Battles of Ypres	April 22-May 25, 1915	
Gallipoli and Dardanelles Campaign	April 22, 1915-January 9, 1916	This campaign, which occurred in Turkey, was an abysmal failure and forced Winston Churchill to leave politics for a little while.
Battle of Verdun	February 21-December 13, 1916	An American ambulance driver called Verdun "the slaughterhouse of the world."[8]
Battle of Jutland	May 31-June 1, 1916	The Battle of Jutland was the largest naval battle during World War I.
Battle of the Somme	July 1-November 18, 1916	During this battle, the single-bloodiest day of the war occurred.
Brusilov Offensive	June 4-September 20, 1916	This offensive was the most famous battle of the Eastern Front and was really the only successful Russian offensive.

---

8. Jankowski, 2014.

Famous Battles	Dates of the Battles	Interesting Facts about the Battles
Battle of Passchendaele	July 31-November 10, 1917	This offensive was an Allied attempt to break through to the English Channel.
Kaiserschlacht (Kaiser's Battle)	March 21-April 5, 1918	Known also as the German spring offensives, the Kaiserschlacht was Germany's attempt to gain the upper hand and end the war once and for all.
"Hundred Days" Campaign	August 1-November 11, 1918	This Allied campaign — later called the "Advance to Victory" — began at Amiens, France. It pushed the Germans back to the original lines of 1914, and, ultimately, defeated the Germans.

On the 11th hour of the 11th day of the 11th month (November 11, 1918), the armistice, which the Allies and Germans had signed at 5:12 a.m., took effect and brought an end to one of the deadliest wars the world had ever seen. Two months later, the Paris Peace Conference began on January 18, 1919 to discuss the peace terms for Germany and its allies. Because the Allied governments did not recognize the Bolshevik government, Russia was not invited to the peace conference, and neither were the defeated Central Powers — Germany, Austria-Hungary, Turkey, and Bulgaria.[9] While Germany did attend the proceedings, they were not allowed to take part. Even

9. "The Paris Peace Conference and the Treaty of Versailles."

though 27 nations participated, the "Big Three" — the United Kingdom, France, and the United States — led the discussion. In the end, the conference oversaw the creation and signing of five different treaties with the Central Powers and the brief establishment of the League of Nations.

 Inspired by President Woodrow Wilson's Fourteen Points, the League of Nations was founded in 1920 as a result of the Paris Peace Conference that ended World War I. The League was the first international organization with the primary goal of maintaining world peace. According to Wilson, "A general association of nations must be formed under specific covenants for the purpose of affording mutual guarantees of political independence and territorial integrity to great and small states alike."[10] America, however, did not join the League of Nations, which greatly reduced its appeal, prestige, and success. It existed from 1920 to 1946, although its power waned in the 1930s. In 1946, the United Nations replaced it and took over its duties.

Many believe that the so-called war guilt clauses — Articles 231 and 232 — which required that Germany, as the guilty party, make reparations (the paying of debts) to the Allies led to the rise of Adolf Hitler and the Nazis in the 1930s. Originally, the Germans were required to repay 266 gold marks, or roughly $63 billion — approximately $768 billion in 2018 — but that was later reduced to $33 billion — approximately $402 billion in 2018.[11] In order to make its first payment of $500 million in August 1921, the German government just printed paper money. The government continued to do this, leading first to the hyperinflation of 1923 and later to Hitler who gave the Germans hope again. As Hitler himself noted, "My programme from the first was to abolish the Treaty of Versailles . . . I have written it thousands of times. No human being has ever declared or recorded what he wanted more than me."[12]

---

10. Wilson, 1918.
11. Suddath, 2010.
12. Johnson, 2009.

In the end, World War I caused the deaths of 8.5 million soldiers and at least 6 million civilians. The Western Front, which was the primary focus of the war, had 11 million casualties, over 3 million deaths, and over 7.5 million injuries.[13] Since the majority of the battles in World War I took place on the Western Front in an area about 85 miles wide, over 3 million men died on a plot of land the width of Maryland.

13. "The Great War — Casualties and Deaths."

Chapter 2

On the Home Front

"Will Weeping Mothers Suddenly Dry Their Tears?"

Daughters, Mothers, and Wives: The Unnamed Heroes

If you were born in America, you probably think of World War II as the most devastating war. You might have a grandfather or great-uncle who fought in the war and perhaps did not return. For the French, World War I haunted them for generations, as it touched nearly every family in France. As Charles de Gaulle — the future leader of the French resistance during World War II and a renowned general and statesman — wrote while still a young captain, "Will France be quick to forget her 1.5 million dead, her million dead, her one million mutilated, her destroyed cities? Will weeping mothers suddenly dry their tears? Will orphans stop being orphans, widows being widows?"[14]

The Great War definitely saw some amazing women who served as spies, soldiers, and nurses, but the majority of the women stayed home and watched the destruction of their homes, families, and livelihoods. There is little written about them in history textbooks because they did not accomplish anything astronomical; rather, they were nameless daughters, moth-

---

14. Kladstrup and Kladstrup, 2006.

ers, and wives, known only to their families. And many of them lived in France. Every village in France lost at least one citizen except one.[15] Even today, almost every city, town, and village (no matter how small) lays a wreath to honor the fallen of the Great War.

The popular and widespread vigor that mothers, fathers, and siblings had felt sending their sons and brothers off to war — "The boys will be home by Christmas" — quickly dissipated when the European countryside was soon filled with the blood of the men serving and the civilians left behind. In the Champagne region, the town of Reims experienced desolation just weeks into the war. On September 14, 1914, German artillery began shelling the countryside, forcing many of the champagne producers to hide in the cellars. When Charles Walfard, head of the champagne house of Veuve Ginet, left to help evacuate 30 wounded soldiers from a nearby clinic, nuns directed him to a cellar where a bomb had recently exploded. As Walfard entered the cellar, he stepped into a pit of red liquid, which he originally believed to be blood "only to realize that it was wine from a barrel that had been smashed." When he went to take another step, an obstacle stopped him. Lighting a match revealed the body of a nun who had been hit by shrapnel. Walfard also later discovered the bodies of two more deceased nuns who had been killed by shrapnel and rubble.[16]

Even for those women who did not give their lives, life without their husbands and sons was painful. Since 1900, there had been very few decent harvests and only one good harvest in 1911 in Champagne.[17] The beautiful, ripening grapes of 1914 had to be harvested because many cellars had very little champagne in stock. This task was left to old men, women, and children. As an example, Pol-Roger, a wine house known for its cham-

---

15. Ibid.
16. Ibid.
17. Ibid.

pagnes — which were Winston Churchill's favorite — acutely felt the absence of the vignerons (people who cultivate grapes for winemaking) and came up with a solution to use the people left behind.

Although women like these nuns, grape harvesters, and champagne producers who served in their communities by attending to the wounded and continuing the work of their town are often unnamed, they represent the ethos of the daughters, mothers, and wives who stayed behind on the Home Front. As Josephine Therese, a young American woman in wartime Germany noted, "The [German] women were doing almost everything that the men had done."[18] Matilde Serao, an Italian journalist similarly observed, "While the Italian country man … fought … the Italian country woman worked the land as if she were a man."[19] They were strong in the midst of horrific news like the death of a husband or son. Alan Seeger, an American poet who served in the Great War and died during the Battle of the Somme, wrote in 1915, "Poor ruined villages of Northern France! They lie like so many silent graveyards, each little house the tomb of some scattered family's happiness."[20]

Resisters and Spies: The Shameful Heroes

For some women, keeping up the home and continuing the family work was their contribution to the war effort. For others, they wanted to do more. Some of these women became spies. The German occupation of Belgium — although less brutal during the First World War in contrast to the Second — provided ample opportunity for the Belgians and French to spy for the Allies and the German occupiers to spy on the Allies. No matter what side women infiltrators were on, they always had other jobs. Sometimes they were nurses; other times they were women of ill repute and

18. Atwood, 2016.
19. Ibid.
20. Kladstrup and Kladstrup, 2006.

known for relationships with powerful men. Sometimes they were relatively unknown; other times they were infamous, as in the case of Margaretha Zelle or Mata Hari, perhaps the most well-known female spy in the Great War. In every case, however, they risked their lives and their reputations, as spying was dishonorable, even for men. It is estimated that at least nine and up to 81 women who spied for the Central Powers were caught and later shot by the French during the span of the war.[21] In fact, some people even suggested that women were better spies than men in the Great War:

> In war, truly, the female of the species is more deadly than the male. In all the annals of the great war [sic] that is shaking the world, there is nothing half so fascinating, nor yet half so strange, as the part that the woman spy is playing in the gigantic game that may remake the map of the world.[22]

In addition, Barbara Craydon posited that the female spies of World War I continued a long tradition of feminine prowess in espionage:

> [T]he German female spy, dressed in the last echo of the fashion, is the most dangerous of all of the elements of warfare that have been brought to bear in the great struggle. And she is by no means a creature of modern warfare. Women dared and died for their loves in the old days, when feudal barons ruled at large, and left their own homes, firesides and blood kin to betray a land for love.[23]

Women spies, although not unique to the Great War, certainly played increasingly important roles.

---

21. Atwood, 2016.
22. Craydon, 1918.
23. Craydon, 1918.

Mata Hari in 1915

 The extent to which women would devote themselves to spying sometimes bordered on the absurd. Ida Mullerthal, in love with Johann Schorveder, allowed him to tattoo her back with India ink with the fortification plans for Posen, part of the German Empire. Her elaborate tattoo included the emplacements, the gun positions, and the munitions stations of the post.[24]

---

24. Ibid.

Louise de Bettignies: "Queen of the Spies"

Louise de Bettignies, who had received an offer to tutor the children of Archduke Franz Ferdinand as a young woman, created an extensive spy network that provided information to the British and the MI6 intelligence service, all based in her hometown of Lille in the north of France. Bettignies first came to the attention of both the British and French intelligence agencies through the "family post," in which she served as the messenger, delivering information to family members outside occupied France. Using lemon juice, which is an inexpensive invisible ink, Bettignies covered a large petticoat with messages. Once she got to her destination, she would iron the petticoat and deliver the messages.

Louise de Bettignies

The British foreign intelligence service, Secret Intelligence Service (SIS), was founded in 1909. It acquired its current name in 1920, and was officially acknowledged in 1994. It is commonly known as MI6, which means Military Intelligence, Section 6.

On her journey back from England to unoccupied France, both the British and French approached Bettignies. She opted to spy for the British because they would pay her during the war. Delivering the last messages, Bettignies returned to England to begin training. When Bettignies returned to Lille, she began establishing an intelligence network, which became known as the "Alice network" due to her alias, Alice Dubois. Bettignies had hundreds of people in her network from her "lieutenant" (second-in-command) Marie-Léonie Vanhoutte, given the code name Charlotte Lameron, to Victor Viaene, known as Albert, to Mme Levengle.

When Bettignies received information, she summarized the material into a report and determined how to get it out of the occupied areas as quickly as possible. The British army and intelligence agency needed the most current information available. Bettignies sometimes took the information herself to England, although there were a variety of couriers in the network. They made sure that they could dispose of the reports quickly if needed. Sometimes they would attach the message to a string so that they could throw it out of their bag if searched and then follow the string back to the message.[25] Extremely successful at her work, Bettignies believed that the Germans were too stupid to realize what was going on. Arrested on October 20, 1915, Bettignies was taken to prison for five months, tried in court, and received a death sentence, which was later commuted (reduced) to life imprisonment after the public outrage regarding Edith Cavell's death (discussed further in the next section). Unfortunately, Bettignies did not live to see the end of the war. She died on September 27, 1918 after an

---

25. Atwood, 2016.

unsuccessful operation — likely due to the filth of the prison — to remove a cancerous tumor. Her legacy, however, was established. Thanks to Bettignies's "Alice Network," the British gained substantial amounts of valuable intelligence, including information about German preparations for the Battle of Verdun. Both the commander of the British Expeditionary Force in France, Sir John French, and members of the British intelligence agency spoke highly of Bettignies. Marshal Ferdinand Foch, Supreme Allied Commander, even conferred the Ordre de l'Armes (a military award) to Bettignies in her absence after first learning of her death sentence and stated that she possessed "a heroism rarely surpassed..."[26]

Edith Cavell: Dedicated Nurse and Spy Condemned to Death

Edith Cavell was perhaps one of the most well-known spies. She had a daytime job as a nurse, which gave her ample opportunity to help Allied soldiers who wandered into Brussels. Born in 1865 in the United Kingdom, Cavell become director of Belgium's first training school for nurses in 1907 after 10 years of nursing experience. When the British forces began to retreat after a brief battle with the Germans at Mons, 30 miles from Brussels, in August 1914, some British soldiers were cut off from their units. If the Germans found them before they made it back to their units, the British soldiers would immediately be taken to prisoner of war camps. Fortunately for some Allied soldiers, they found assistance through Edith Cavell and others in Brussels. Cavell was able to use her occupation as a nurse as a ruse to save countless Allied soldiers.

From November 1, 1914, when she assisted two British men, to August 3, 1915, when she was captured and imprisoned, Edith helped Allied soldiers — Belgian, British, and French — escape detection from the Germans. Although Cavell had others in her network, including Princess

---

26. Hoehling, 1992.

Marie de Croÿ, she frequently escorted the men to transfer points in Brussels herself:

> She would pretend to be merely taking her dog for a walk, using various routes, while the soldiers — disguised as Belgian farmers or miners — followed her from a distance until they made contact with the waiting guide.[27]

While Cavell threw herself wholeheartedly into helping as many Allied soldiers escape as possible, she still maintained a strong interest in nursing and caring for as many wounded soldiers as possible, even Germans.

Edith Cavell (center) with student nurses she trained in Brussels.

Although the 1906 Geneva Convention normally guaranteed medical personnel protection, this right was forfeited if medical activities were used as a cover for belligerent actions. While Cavell had not taken up nursing in order to spy for and protect the Allies, she did use her occupation as a

---

27. Atwood, 2016.

cover, thus putting herself in jeopardy of imprisonment and execution. After Cavell's arrest on August 3, 1915, based on the charge of harboring Allied soldiers, she admitted that she had conveyed 60 British soldiers, 15 French soldiers, and 100 French and Belgian civilians to the frontier and opened up her home to them.[28] Held in prison for 10 weeks — in which Cavell spent most of her time preparing for death by reading the Bible and Thomas à Kempis' "The Imitation of Christ," Cavell was court-martialed for aiding enemy soldiers crossing the Belgian frontier. According to German military law, conducting soldiers to the enemy was punishable by death for both Germans and foreigners. Cavell was found guilty.

On October 11, 1915, the night before Cavell's execution, Reverend Stirling Gahan, an Anglican chaplain, came to see her and administer Holy Communion, as Cavell was a dedicated Anglican. While speaking with Reverend Gahan that evening, Cavell stated her now famous words, which were later inscribed on her statue in St. Martin's Place in London:

> Standing as I do in view of God and eternity, I realize that patriotism is not enough. I must have no hatred or bitterness towards anyone.[29]

At 7:00 a.m. the next morning, two firing squads of eight men each carried out Cavell's sentence and shot her and Philippe Baucq at the Belgian Tir National Shooting Range in Schaebeek.

Within days of Cavell's execution, the world erupted at the news of a woman being shot. Because the Germans experienced such indignation at the execution of Edith Cavell, they resolved not to execute other females in the future without the consent of the Kaiser, the German king. In fact,

---

28. Chisholm, 1922.
29. King, 1917.

Kaiser Wilhelm II altered the sentence of three women from execution to life imprisonment after the public outcry.[30] Thus, Cavell's death may have saved countless other women.

Everyone had different opinions about Cavell's death. Some believed that Cavell deserved to be shot for violating a law, regardless of whether she was a woman. Others suggested that Cavell should have received some mercy as a female. For many American men, it was inconceivable that the Germans would kill a woman. They believed that was unjust and an improper way to treat a woman. As George W. Kirchwey observed,

> According to strict military law, Edith Cavell is guilty, and the fact that she is a woman should not be taken into consideration; but from the viewpoint of humanity and public opinion it seems to me that her execution was absolutely unjustified. It has been the practice of all nations to apply the rules of war less vigorously to women than to men, even though the offence [sic] committed be technically the same, and I think this policy is sound.[31]

Some women, often suffragists, may have disagreed with Cavell's execution, but argued that it was not out of pity or that she was a woman that she should not have been killed. They believed that there was a clear connection between men who protested Cavell's execution and then ignored women's pleas for equal rights. As Leta Hollingsworth, psychologist at Bellevue Hospital, stated, "There is no question that a man who is strong for special privileges [regarding avoiding execution for crimes committed] for a woman is strong for keeping her from her rights."[32] Mrs. Charles Stevenson —who served as a Red Cross nurse during the Spanish-American War

---

30. Atwood, 2016.
31. Dunbar, 1915.
32. Ibid.

of 1898 and later became vice-president of the New York State Nurses' Association — concurred with Hollingsworth: "It is true that men who might deny women simple rights would have excused Edith Cavell on the ground that she was a woman. This is natural at all times, and especially in the case of a nurse."[33] By contrast, women like Hollingsworth noted that technically Cavell did break the law and deserved execution just like a man would. These women believed that it would be wrong to pardon Cavell just because she was a woman.

Others, like Lillian Wald, noted that Cavell deserved death if she were a spy, but if she were just a nurse helping a variety of people, that did not merit death. Even so, Wald echoed the sentiments of other women that Cavell should not have been pardoned solely on the basis of her womanhood:

> On the whole, the killing of Edith Cavell is just a part of the general horror and may be classed with the invasion of Belgium and the sinking of the Lusitania. We are shocked to our marrow by the loss of this splendid woman, this valuable nurse, who is as highly esteemed here as in England, and who cared for Germans as well as her own people. Now, if she merely, as a faithful, competent nurse, helped prisoners escape, that is a part of the tenderness and compassion of nursing, and there isn't a woman living who would not have done the same. But if she was engaged by the government as a spy, that is a different matter. She took her chances and she should not have escaped because she was a woman. Which was the case I do not know. I do know that whatever the reason for her death, whether it was justified or not by the laws of war, it is one of the most convincing proofs that war should be abolished.[34]

---

33. Ibid.
34. Ibid.

As noted before, nursing was an acceptable occupation for women, but spying was not. Wald's opinions clearly indicate how strongly individuals felt about the caring role women should have in society, the dishonorable role of subterfuge in war, and the unnecessariness of war.

Finally, still others pointed to Cavell's execution as just another example of the horrors of Germany. According to Elizabeth Jordan of Harper & Brothers, Germany revealed her true colors of brutality and lack of civilization through the execution of Cavell:

> During this war Germany has committed three appalling outrages, which, from every point of view, are also three appalling blunders — the invasion of Belgium, the destruction of the Lusitania, and the execution of Edith Cavell. She [Germany] has tried to justify each of these, and in every attempt she has shown a horrified world the vulnerable spot in her mighty armor — the quality which, great as she is, must lead to her ultimate defeat. No nation which performs and defends such actions can long survive; no such nation can triumph over the civilized peoples of the earth. For Germany is undermining her own social structure as well as the world's; she is tearing away from beneath her the splendid foundation of civilization and the high ideals which her own people built. That the many high-minded and heroic Germans should suffer for the blindness and blunders of the few is the real tragedy of the Fatherland.[35]

One must remember that the United States had not joined the Great War at this time — America would not join until April 2, 1917. As a result, Jordan did not have any particular reason to dislike the Germans other than the fact that the United States and Britain had a special connection. Thus,

---

35. Dunbar, 1915.

Jordan's sentiments against the Germans are more than simply nationalist fervor against the other side. It is also interesting to note how confident Jordan was that the Germans would ultimately lose the war, even when the early years of World War I were certainly Germany's strongest times.

 Some American suffragists used the execution of Edith Cavell to argue for women's right to vote, which was not passed in the U.S. Congress until 1919 and ratified until 1920. Olive Stott Gabriel, president of the Women Lawyers' Association, observed,

> I am strong for women, but I am stronger for justice. If women have a voice in lawmaking, they won't need any special privileges. They will take care of themselves. The crime against Edith Cavell was not in executing her, but the fact that she had no voice in the laws that governed her.[36]

In Gabriel's estimation, men should not pity that Cavell died but rather that she and other women did not have an equal right to vote.

Cavell's execution transformed the German response to female spies and certainly increased the success of other women who followed in Cavell's footsteps. As prolific American novelist Gertrude Atherton noted about Cavell's character,

> As for Edith Cavell, she knew what she was about. She knew war; she knew the Germans. She kept her wits till the last, we are told. She probably did not look so far ahead as to know that her death would have this wonderful recruiting value which it has had, but I have no doubt she did know it would rebound to her country's benefit and to Germany's detriment.[37]

---

36. Ibid.
37. Ibid.

Marthe Cnockaert: Double-Agent (for a couple days!)

Marthe Cnockaert was a Belgian woman who moved to Rousselaere, a Belgian town close to the fighting, in January 1915 and began to work as a nurse in the hospital, serving both wounded Belgians and Germans. Cnockaert desperately wanted to play a more active role in the war, but as a woman, her options were limited. Cnockaert's first split-second reaction to family friend Lucelle Deldonck asking if she wanted to serve her country, which Cnockaert knew meant spying, was one of horror. Spying was underhanded and tricky, and Cnockaert did not know if she wanted to be a part of that. After a moment's hesitation, Cnockaert regained her composure and agreed. Deldonck informed Cnockaert that an agent of the British Intelligence would soon contact her. As Cnockaert remembers in her autobiography, she took to spying because she wanted to do more for the war effort, for her country: "Because I am a woman I could not serve my country as a soldier. I took the only course open to me."[38] Cnockaert is a unique example of a spy because she actually ended up briefly living as a double-agent, spying for both Great Britain and Germany!

Three days after being approached by Deldonck about serving her country, Cnockaert met her contact, an old woman who sold vegetables, known as "Canteen Ma" to the Germans. After trying to sell Cnockaert vegetables, "Canteen Ma" slipped Cnockaert a piece of paper telling her to meet up with Lisette, who turned out to be Deldonck. Cnockaert's role as a nurse serving both Belgians and Germans near the front line gave her ample opportunity to spy, so the British Intelligence would rely on Cnockaert to provide information about troop movements, ammunitions dumps, and so on. Deldonck let Cnockaert know that a British resister, identified by two safety pins under his collar, would soon contact Cnockaert about her first assignment.

---

38. McKenna, 2015.

The man with two safety pins gave Cnockaert her first message, which she delivered to "Number 63" by tapping three times on a designated window, waiting, and then tapping two more times. Two months of delivering messages like this first one flew by, and Cnoackert received a new opportunity in March 1915. Cnoackert's father became the owner of a café in Rousselaere, which three Germans had taken to frequenting. Cnoackert thought that by picking up extra hours working at the café, she might be able to discover additional information to pass along to the British Intelligence. The three German men, particularly Otto von Promft, were quite pleasant and enjoyable, so it was no surprise that Cnockaert received a surprise visit from a safety pin man warning her that these Germans had been specifically sent to find out spies.

When the hospital chief doctor, the Oberatz, asked Cnockaert to visit him in his office, Cnockaert worried that she had been found out. Instead, to her pleasant surprise, she learned that she was receiving the Iron Cross for her "fine work" at the hospital.[39] This award ingratiated Cnockaert to Otto von Promft, who believed that Cnockaert supported the Central Powers, and he asked her — in a similar way to Deldonck — if she wanted to serve the Fatherland. At first unsure, Cnockaert later agreed and provided some information that would not jeopardize the Allies. When von Promft questioned Cnockaert on the authenticity of the evidence, she quickly informed the safety pin man. Soon after, von Promft was found dead with two bullet wounds to the head. At the very least, Cnockaert did not have to worry about being a double agent anymore!

 **DID YOU KNOW?** The British and French governments attempted to use aerial bombardments to kill German Kaiser Wilhelm II during World War I. In July 1915, Cnockaert began to notice the Germans in Rousselaere suddenly working very hard to make the city look good, including issuing new uniforms. Cnockaert learned from her fellow British spies that the Kaiser was planning a visit and succeeded in acquiring the exact date

---

39. Ibid.

from an enamored German officer: July 24, 1915. Unfortunately for Cnockaert and the Allies, however, the Kaiser cancelled the trip because the Allies had been bombing the surrounding areas quite frequently in the weeks leading up to his planned visit.[40]

The fall of 1916 brought an end to Cnockaert's time working at the hospital and spying for the Allies. Some new German nurses were assigned to the hospital in October 1916 and did not get along with Cnockaert. She opted to resign, and the Oberatz felt sad to see her go. In November 1916, Cnockaert's carelessness got her arrested. Cnockaert and several others had placed explosives in a German ammo dump, and she lost her watch, which had her initials engraved on the back, in the debris. Unaware where she had misplaced her watch, Cnockaert fell into a trap. After reading a notice board listing stolen items, including her watch, she retrieved it. Because the Germans had discovered the watch in the debris of the bombed ammo dump, they had enough information to suspect Cnockaert. They rushed to Cnockaert's apartment and ruthlessly searched her belongings, finding two coded messages that Cnockaert had sloppily hidden.

In November 1916, Cnockaert was tried, but she received a lighter sentence due to her admirable work with Germans and Belgians in the hospital. The Oberatz even testified on Cnockaert's behalf, noting that she had received the Iron Cross. Unlike Cavell, Cnockaert was not condemned to death, but rather to life in prison. Cnockaert would remain in prison until the end of the war when she was liberated by British troops. After the war, Cnockaert married a British soldier, John McKenna, and the couple moved to England during World War II where Cnockaert died in 1966. As Winston Churchill himself observed, "Marthe McKenna...fulfilled in every respect the conditions which make the terrible profession of a spy dignified and honourable."[41]

---

40. Suddaby, 2007.
41. McKenna, 2015.

Chapter 3

On the Front

"No Woman Has Gone There Yet"

Journalists: The Investigative Heroes

While spying was seen as a disreputable activity, especially for women, journalism was surprisingly even more challenging for women. In the early 20th century, very few women were journalists, and war journalism had just begun to develop. Women who wanted to step outside of the traditional roles of wives and mothers became known as "New Women" and had just enough gumption to break into the male-dominated profession of war journalism.[42] Although women were not allowed to officially report for the military due to their gender, they found other ways to get to the front. Sometimes they would report on the woman's side of the war, namely hospitals and homes. Others dressed up as men and joined the military. No matter what angle the women selected, however, they all wanted to discover what was really occurring on the battlefields. For many women, they saw it as a moral duty to report what was happening.

It was hardest for a woman to get to the Western Front to report, and most governments did not like women reporting. In two instances, however,

---

42. "1914-1918: WWI – Women Reporters," 2018.

women received the go-ahead to come and report: the unoccupied section of Belgium and the Eastern Front in Russia.[43] In the first case, German propaganda had been intense in Belgium, and the Allies welcomed people who would tell the truth about the German invasion of Belgium. For the latter, the Tsar, in a push to stay in World War I, encouraged reporters to come and observe the Eastern Front, including the famous Women's Battalion of Death. Some journalists even stayed long enough to witness the Bolshevik Revolution of October 1917.

Even if women were able to get to the frontlines, it was extremely challenging for them as women. Reporter Corra Horris noted: "[B]eing banned from the front because of their sex proved to be the biggest obstacle to women journalists [in terms of professional advancement]."[44] Harris also observed that like the daughters, mothers, and wives, women journalists were also often unsung heroes: "Men's sacrifice in war is at least recorded by history…while women's story goes untold."[45]

Madeleine Zabriskie Doty: Feminist and Journalist

Madeleine Zabriskie Doty wore many hats: she was a journalist, lawyer, pacifist, social reformer, suffragist, and teacher. Doty began her career writing about prison reform in New York City, but when World War I began, she longed to report overseas. Three months after the Great War started in August 1914, Doty founded the Women's Peace Party (WPP) in November 1914, America's first all-female peace organization.

In 1915, Doty, Jane Addams, and other American women traveled to the International Congress of Women at The Hague in the Netherlands. At first, the New York Evening Post and The Century Magazine asked Doty to attend

---

43. Atwood, 2016.
44. "1914-1918: WWI – Women Reporters," 2018.
45. Ibid.

the congress as a correspondent, which the staunch feminist and pacifist did. As Doty recalled in her book, the women at the international congress wanted to bring peace on earth: "The women knew they couldn't stop the war, but they decided to register a protest against the slaughter of man and lay plans for a future permanent peace."[46] Later, The New York Tribune requested that Doty travel to Germany and report on the conditions there. Doty stayed in Germany for a little while and then spent some time in France and England.

Doty's investigative and observing tendencies served her well in her depictions of Germany, England, and France. As she aptly stated,

> The wounded do not like to talk war. Their experiences have been too terrible. They try to forget. War is no longer a series of gallant deeds; it is a matter of bursting shells. One man with leg blown off had never seen the enemy.[47]

Soldiers even told Doty that they did not want to have children so that they would not have to see what they had seen.

Quite perceptive, Doty predicted that Germany would fight hard until the end:

> For Germany will never give in. She will fight to her last man. If pushed to the wall, all the bitterness and fear that have crept into the nation will be directed toward a gigantic effort to blow up the world…Germany, the land of the Christmas-tree, and folk songs, and fireside, and gay childish laughter, turned into a relentless fighting machine![48]

---

46. Doty, 1917.
47. Ibid.
48. Ibid.

Doty's time in Berlin, the capital city of Germany, had definitely given her insight into the country.

When Doty was back in England, the editor at The New York Tribune, however, desired more information and asked Doty to return to Germany. At first skeptical, Doty later accepted when the editor stated that he wanted someone who would tell the truth and believed that Doty, as a neutral individual, would be an excellent candidate. As Doty remembered, "That settled it. To be asked to tell the truth is a proposition not to reject."[49] Doty's second trip to Germany included meeting a variety of Social Democrats and talking with Germans who desired peace. When Doty intended to cross from the German border into Switzerland, Doty quickly realized that the German authorities might seize her notes from her travels and began to copy them onto tissue paper and then hid them on the inside of her coat, thus saving the notes and making it possible for her to write articles when she returned to America.

 Social Democrats want to see a fusion of socialism (government regulating the means of production) with political democracy (all people are represented in the government). Social Democrats encourage government involvement in the economy and society for social justice initiatives while still maintaining a democratic government and a capitalist society. The most popular Social Democratic Party, which is still in existence, is in Germany.

When Doty returned to the United States after her travels in France, Great Britain, and Germany, she published "Short Rations: An American Woman in Germany, 1915-1916." Just months later, Doty traveled to Russia to report on the Russian Revolution and also visited Japan and other countries, which she discussed in "Behind the Battle Line: Around the World in 1918." As a devoted pacifist, Doty served on a committee for the League of Nations,

---

49. Ibid.

and, as a dedicated feminist, Doty wrote for The Suffragist magazine and served on the National Advisory Council for the National Women's Party.

 During Doty's second trip to Germany, she spent much time with Social Democrats. As a pacifist, Doty was inspired by the famous Social Democrat Rosa Luxembourg who had rushed into the middle of the street filled with soldiers urging them not to shoot their brothers.[50] Before Doty left Germany, she traveled four hours to hear Clara Zetkin speak. Zetkin was a Social Democrat who was also passionate about women's rights, including initiating the idea of an International Women's Day. As Doty herself described Zetkin, "[Clara Zetkin] is a blazing comet — over 60, with white hair and shaken with illness, she fights on."[51]

In 1919, Doty married Roger Baldwin who helped found the American Civil Liberties Union (ACLU), but separated from him in 1925 and divorced him in 1935. In 1925, Doty had taken a two-year position as the international secretary for the Women's International League for Peace and Freedom in Geneva, Switzerland. Doty would spend the majority of the rest of her life in Switzerland, including founding and directing two programs for American college juniors to prepare for international work known as Junior Year in Geneva — which is still in existence today! After receiving a doctorate degree in International Relations from the University of Geneva in 1945, Doty spent most of her time teaching and writing in Switzerland, although she died in October 1963 in Greenfield, Massachusetts.[52]

Dorothy Lawrence: Sapper and Journalist

Rejected first as a civilian employee of the Voluntary Aid Detachment (VAD) and then as a freelance war correspondent, Englishwoman Dor-

---

50. Atwood, 2016.
51. Doty, 1917.
52. Hall, 2018.

othy Lawrence decided to take matters into her own hands. As Lawrence stated to a few Frenchmen in Crecil, France who had won her confidence before she was rejected as a freelance war correspondent in Senils, "I want to go right into the firing-line."[53] After these rejections, Lawrence remained steadfast:

> I'll see what an ordinary English girl, without credentials or money, can accomplish. If war correspondents cannot get out there, I'll see whether I cannot go one better than these big men with their cars, credentials, and money.[54]

With the help of 10 British Army soldiers, whom she called her "Khaki accomplices," Lawrence was able to piece together a uniform and forged papers identifying her as Private Denis Smith.

Lawrence even shaved her face with a razor in the hopes that she would be able to grow facial hair. She never did! Although many of the soldiers who knew Lawrence was a woman assumed that she just wanted to go to the front because she was a "camp follower," or a prostitute, Lawrence recalled in her memoirs that no man ever harmed her. Lawrence kept a heavy military knife on her person, though, just in case she needed it!

As Lawrence headed to the front, she realized that she needed to find a soldier who approximated her height in order to blend in, which she did. Fortunately for Lawrence, the man, Tom Dunn, had been watching her and was willing to help her even though he knew that she was a woman. Dunn was a sapper, someone who digs tunnels, and offered to not only take care of Lawrence but also teach her how to be a sapper.

---

53. Lawrence, 1919.
54. Lawrence, 1919.

Dorothy Lawrence in a male soldier's uniform

Lawrence unhappily became sick after being exposed to incessant fire for 10 days and being on the front for two months. Lawrence decided to report herself to the sergeant, hoping that he would not reveal her identity. She was wrong. Not only did the sergeant report that Lawrence was a woman but he also accused her of being a spy and wanted to arrest her in the king's name. Upset that the sergeant had betrayed her, Lawrence retorted, "Before this arrest takes place I wish to make it clear that I am not a spy. I am an English girl."[55]

Before long, Lawrence was interrogated by a variety of military officers, all of whom continued to believe that she was a spy, and ended up in the Divisional Headquarters, where she received a private court-martial. Cross-examination, however, was not finished; the officers intended to move Lawrence to the General Headquarters in St. Omer. Along the way, they stopped at a convent where Lawrence stayed for two weeks until Lord French gave orders that Lawrence should return to England. (A judge had desired that Lawrence remain in France until the end of the Battle of Loos because he believed that she might disclose confidential information.) While in the convent, Lawrence signed a document that forbid her to write about her experiences. When she arrived in London as a "prisoner of war" — the British military still believed Lawrence to be a spy —she waited in the hall of the Scotland Yard for a plainsclothes detective to reappear, expecting that she would have to face yet another interrogation. Lawrence was wrong. The detective returned and stated, "All right, you need not come in…Go not, but for [10] days keep us notified of your address."[56]

 Sometimes it can be unclear as to what exactly is meant by "the front." Lawrence wrote about this exact issue in her book:

Nobody here at home realizes quite what "the front" signifies. To womenfolk that word implies one narrow line, called the fighting-line, with only such towns as fringe it. In reality the front embraces vast stretches of country, often miles away from the cannon-mouth, and without any scenes of excitement.[57]

---

55. Ibid.
56. Ibid.
57. Ibid.

Lawrence was free, but she was not free to write. As Lawrence noted herself about the affidavit in which she promised not to write, "In making that promise I sacrificed the chance of earning by newspaper articles written on this escapade, as a girl compelled to earn her livelihood."[58] She attempted to publish some articles about the war in The Wide World Magazine, but was silenced by the War Office. When she published her book "Sapper Dorothy Lawrence" in 1919, it was well-received in England and the United States, but was heavily censored by the War Office in Great Britain.

Unfortunately, Lawrence never made it as a journalist, despite the extent to which she went to report during World War I, and sadly went insane after the age of 30. Reportedly raped by a church guardian when she was younger and with no family to take care of her, a doctor sent Lawrence to London County Mental Hospital in Hanwell and later to what is now known as Friern Hospital, where Lawrence died in 1964.[59]

Mary Roberts Rinehart: American Agatha Christie and War Journalist

When American Mary Roberts Rinehart traveled across the Atlantic to get a first-hand account of World War I, she had already published five books, two plays, and countless short stories. Rinehart's "The Circular Staircase," published in 1907, elevated her to success. During Christmas 1914, when Christmas Truces were taking place all over the Western Front, Rinehart received her own Christmas gift: The Saturday Evening Post would finance her trip overseas to visit the front.[60]

---

58. Ibid.
59. Marzouk, 2003.
60. MacLeod, 2016.

Mary Roberts Rinehart in 1914

Armed with a letter of introduction to Lord Northcliffe from the Post's editor George Horace Lorimer, Rinehart arrived in London in January 1915. Northcliffe, a well-known British publisher, informed Rinehart that she likely would not be able to visit the front as hundreds of journalists were stuck in London with the same aspirations. That did not stop Rinehart. She contacted the Anglo-Belgian committee of the Belgian Red Cross, headquartered in London, and asked to see the front: "Let me see conditions as they really are…It is no use telling me about them. Let me see them. Then I can tell the American people what they have already done in the war zone, and what they may be asked to do."[61] As a young woman, Rinehart had nurses' training, so she convinced the committee that she would be the perfect candidate to report on the conditions on the front. When asked where she wanted go, Rinehart replied, "Everywhere," and she received

---

61. Rinehart, 1915.

letters of introduction to a variety of Belgian military officers as well as a special residency card that allowed Rinehart to move freely between the two countries without having to apply for a new permit.[62] As she traveled throughout Belgium, Rinehart noticed the sad state of the hospitals and the horrors of trench life. But she also noted the responses of the soldiers:

> [T]he little Belgian soldier is a cheery soul. He asks very little, is never surly. A little food, a little sleep — on straw, in a stable or a church — and he is happy again. Over and over, as I saw the Belgian Army, I was impressed with its cheerfulness under unparalleled conditions.[63]

As an author who had already written several books, Rinehart was able to depict vividly the conditions on the front and the men who served:

> Germany's militarism, England's navalism, Russia's autocracy, France, graft-ridden in high places and struggling for rehabilitation after a century of war — and, underneath it all, bearing it on bent shoulders, men like this German prisoner, alone in his room and puzzling it out!

In addition to touring the Belgian hospitals for three weeks, Rinehart also had the opportunity to join a group of journalists traveling to the front. As Rinehart herself stated, "I am to go the firing line. No woman has gone there yet."[64] Rinehart even walked out into no-man's-land with the contingent and later discovered that the officer in charge would never have allowed a woman in no-man's-land had he discovered before Rinehart was already out there. Since the officer realized too late, he could not call out because it would have informed the Germans that the Belgians were there.

---

62. Atwood, 2016.
63. Rinehart, 1915.
64. Rinehart, 1915.

The special residency card that Rinehart received was a pink card that only three people before Rinehart had received: the Belgian King Albert, the Belgian Minister of War, and the premier. Rinehart was the fourth person, first woman, and first non-Belgian to receive the pink card.[65]

Before Rinehart journeyed home, she had the opportunity to interview a variety of famous individuals: Belgian King Albert, Belgian Queen Elizabeth, British Queen Mary, General Ferdinand Foch, and Lord of the Admiralty Winston Churchill. Rinehart's interview with King Albert was supposed to last only 10 minutes, but they ended up speaking for over an hour. As Rinehart described in her book, King Albert was "a very courteous gentleman, with the eyes of one who loves the sea."[66] The king spoke quite openly about the Germans' brutality in their invasion of Belgium, and Rinehart composed an article about the invasion, hoping to motivate American political leaders like President Woodrow Wilson to change America's neutral stance toward the war. Rinehart, unfortunately, was unsuccessful.

 Going to the front gave men and women a new impression of the war. As the final sentence of her book, Mary Roberts Rinehart gives a poignant and apt description of war:

> War is not two great armies meeting in a clash and frenzy of battle. It is much more than that. War is a boy carried on a stretcher, looking up at God's blue sky with bewildered eyes that are soon to close; war is a woman carrying a child that has been wounded by a shell; war is spirited horses tied in burning buildings and waiting for death; war is the flower of a race, torn, battered, hungry, bleeding, up to its knees in icy water; war is an old woman burning a candle before Mater Dolorosa for the son she has given.[67]

65. MacLeod, 2016.
66. Ibid.
67. Rinehart, 1915.

When Rinehart returned to America two months after she arrived in England and Belgium, she published 10 articles about the war and increased the readership of the Post by 50,000.[68] In addition to compiling her observations into a book — "Kings, Queen and Pawns" — Rinehart also let the London Times publish her work. When America joined the war in 1917, the Post asked Rinehart to compose an article encouraging American women to send their sons to war, which Rinehart entitled The Altar of Freedom: "Because I am a woman, I cannot die for my country, but I am doing a far harder thing. I am giving a son to the service of his country, the land he loves."[69] The article backfired, however, as many mothers who had lost sons sent upset and angry letters to Rinehart. As a result, Rinehart adopted a pacifist stance toward World War II. She later wanted to go overseas to report on the front again, but she was too frail to travel as she had a heart condition. By the time America joined World War II, Rinehart supported the war effort by composing articles and encouraging those on the home front to get involved. Rinehart died in New York City in 1958, having lived 82 rich years.

Nurses and Medical Personnel: The Caring Heroes

Beyond living as daughters, mothers, and wives of soldiers, the most prominent role that women held in World War I was as nurses and medical personnel. When the war broke out on August 4, 1914, Dr. Flora Murray and Louisa Garrett Anderson founded the Women's Hospital Corps (WHC).[70] Another doctor, Elsie Inglis, wanted to join the WHC, but there was not room for her. Rather than get frustrated, Dr. Inglis founded the Scottish Women's Hospitals (SWH) Committee, with the first hospital established in Calais, France in December 1914.[71] Later in the month, units were sent to France and Serbia. Over 1,500 women and 20 men worked at the 14 Scottish Women's Hospi-

---

68. Atwood, 2016.
69. Rinehart, 1917.
70. Powell, 2016.
71. Ibid.

tals during World War I.[72] Throughout the course of the war, Scottish Women's Hospitals would serve hundreds of thousands of wounded civilians and soldiers in Corsica, France, Romania, Russia, Salonika, and Serbia.

 The women who served in the Voluntary Aid Detachments became known as the Very Adorable Darlings.

For those who did not have as much nursing experience, there was another option: Voluntary Aid Detachments (VAD). After the war began in August 1914, the British Red Cross and St. John's Ambulance merged and became VADs. Within a couple months, over 46,000 women from a variety of backgrounds joined the VADs: upper class women, suffragists, feminists, and married women.[73] If women were untrained when they first joined, they were given more menial duties, working as cleaners, drivers, and orderlies and were given more duties like supplying food and medical dressings and preparing and cleaning the hospitals as the war went on.[74]

Throughout the war, thousands of women served as nurses and medical personnel from the roughly 60,000 British VAD nurses and 60,000 French nurses to 92,000 German and over 25,000 Russian nurses.[75] Due to 19th century tradition, many of the nurses' uniforms resembled nun's habits, which also served to distance them from the soldiers.[76] Sometimes, however, women had other uniforms, as in the case of the Scottish Women's Hospitals: a gray coat and skirt with Gordon tartan facings.[77] Although they had always been close to the battlefields, nurses worked increasingly closer to the trenches as the war raged on, trying to save as many men as possible. Since women in most coun-

72. "Elsie Inglis to be commemorated for war achievements," 2017.

73. Powell, 2016.

74. Ibid.

75. Atwood, 2016.

76. Ibid.

77. Powell, 2016.

tries could not serve in the military, they saw nursing as their equivalent to military service. As Olive Dent, who served in a VAD on the coast of France and nursed the wounded from the Battle of the Somme, observed, "[T]he New Army of men would need a New Army of nurses. Why not go and learn to be a nurse while the Kitchener men were learning to be soldiers?"[78]

World War I VAD recruitment poster

 Created at the outbreak of World War I, the New Army was initially an all-volunteer army. It was formed on the recommendation of Lord Kitchener, the Secretary of War. Often referred to as Kitchener's Army, or

---

78. Dent, 2014.

disparagingly as Kitchener's Mob, the New Army first saw action at the Battle of Loos (September-October 1915).

Vera Brittain: VAD Nurse and Pacifist

Born as the only daughter of Thomas and Edith Brittain, Vera Brittain and her only sibling, Edward, grew up in a well-to-do family that owned paper mills in Hanley and Cheddleton. 1913 was a significant year for Brittain. Her beloved brother Edward introduced his sister to Roland Leighton, one of his friends from Uppingham School. Roland and Vera quickly developed a close connection. All three of them applied for and were accepted to study in different colleges at Oxford University — English Literature at Somerville College for Vera, Merton College for Leighton, and New College for Edward — and they planned to attend in 1914.

 Brittain's father originally discouraged his daughter from attending college because he believed that it was an unacceptable step for a woman; she should instead prepare for marriage. In 1912, Brittain began attending a course of lectures given by historian John Marriott. After Leighton met Brittain, he began to encourage her to attend university. By 1914, Brittain had successfully persuaded her father, and he relented, allowing her to attend Oxford University.

Edward Brittain and Leighton never made it to Oxford. In August 1914, the Great War broke out, and the young men enlisted in the military. Vera, however, attended Oxford University as planned. In 1915, Edward introduced Vera to one of his friends, Geoffrey Thurlow, who was recovering from shell shock in England. Likely due to her interactions with Thurlow, Vera worked as a nursing assistant at Devonshire Hospital in Buxton during the summer of 1915. While Leighton was on leave in August 1915, he and Vera became engaged. Soon thereafter, Vera began work as a VAD nurse in November 1915 at the First London General Hospital at Camberwell. She served throughout the war, including in Malta and on the front in France.

Vera Brittain and Leighton communicated predominantly via letters and did not get to see each other very often during their courtship and engagement. They met for a grand total of 17 days during their relationship.[79] As Brittain remembered in her autobiography,

> At the beginning of 1915 I was more deeply and ardently in love than I have ever been or am ever likely to be, yet at that time Roland [Leighton] and I had hardly been alone together, and never at all without the constant possibility of observation and interruption.[80]

Leighton's mother referred to Edward, Geoffrey, and Roland as the three musketeers, and their friendship sustained Vera throughout the war. She also would become close with another friend of Edward's named Victor Richardson. Unfortunately, all three men met tragic ends before the war ended.

As the holiday season of 1915 approached, Brittain eagerly awaited the arrival of Leighton, who was to come home on leave. Sadly, Brittain received a call with news of his death, rather than news of his arrival, just before Christmas 1915.

The other three men survived until 1917. Thurlow was killed in an attack on the Scarpe in the spring of 1917; Richardson at first survived a head wound — even though he was blinded — but unexpectedly deteriorated in June 1917 and died; and Edward Brittain died just months before the Armistice on the Italian Front, as the telegram announced: "Regret to inform you Captain E H Brittain M.C. killed in action Italy June 15th."[81]

---

79. Day, 2013.
80. Brittain, 2009.
81. Ibid.

Edward's death was particularly hard on Vera:

> Long after the family had gone to bed and the world had grown
> silent, I crept into the dining room to be alone with Edward's por-
> trait. Carefully closing the door, I turned on the light and looked
> at the pale, pictured face, so dignified, so steadfast, so tragically
> mature. He had been through so much — far, far more than those
> beloved friends who had died at an earlier stage of the interminable
> [endless] War, leaving him alone to mourn their loss.[82]

Armistice Day (November 11, 1918) was particularly hard for Brittain.
Almost everyone in London was rejoicing, but not Brittain. The war had
taken her fiancé, brother, and two close male friends, so all Brittain could
do was mourn the loss of life.

 In 1916, Brittain wrote a letter to her brother Edward
and declared her intentions to write a book if she
survived the war: "If the war spares me, it will be my
one aim to immortalise in a book the story of us four
[Edward, Roland, Vera, and Victor; it was not until later that Vera
became close with Geoffrey]."[83] It took her about 17 years to finish her
book, which Brittain entitled "Testament of Youth." It was based on
the diary she kept throughout most of the war and was an instant hit.
Its first print-run of 3,000 books sold out on the publication day in
August 1933.[84] Storm Jameston commented in the Sunday Times,
"Miss Brittain has written a book which stands alone among books
written by women about the war."[85]

---

82. Brittain, 2009.
83. Day, 2013.
84. Ibid.
85. Brittain, 2009.

Vera Brittain shortly after WWII

After the war, Brittain returned to Oxford and established a friendship with Winifred Holtby until the latter died in 1935. The two women bonded over writing, and Holtby's friendship was a true solace to Brittain as she dealt with the loss of her four friends.

DID YOU KNOW? Brittain wrote 29 books during her 76 years of life. Shirley Williams, Brittain's daughter, remembers the strict writing routine that her mother kept: "sitting down at her typewriter at 10 a.m., having already dealt with her correspondence and bills; at 2 p.m. taking a break when she would lead the children around Battersea Park and recite the Latin names of the birds and flowers; then back to her desk until dinner time."[86]

---

86. Day, 2013.

In the first few years after the war, Brittain never expected to find love again. Fortunately, she was wrong. Brittain married political scientist George Catlin in 1925 and had two children, John and Shirley. She spent much of her life as a staunch pacifist, speaking out against World War II and was in favor of nuclear disarmament during the Cold War. Even though Brittain had a full and happy life, dying at the age of 76, the Great War remained ever in the forefront of her mind, as Brittain's daughter, Shirley Williams, noted:

> It was hard for her to laugh unconstrainedly; at the back of her mind, the row upon row of wooden crosses were planted too deeply. Through her, I learned how much courage it took to live in service to the world when all those one loved best were gone: her fiancé first, her best friend, her beloved only brother. The only salvation was work, particularly the work of patching and repairing those were still alive.[87]

Olive Dent: Elementary School Teacher Turned VAD Nurse

Originally an elementary school teacher, Olive Dent volunteered in her 30s to serve as a nurse in World War I. Before the war, Dent attended courses in hygiene and psychology and worked with St. John's Ambulance, which — as noted above — joined with the British Red Cross to form VADs after the war began.[88] Although some women stayed behind in England and served on the home front, Dent desired to go to the busy war zones in Gallipoli and the Western Front.

In August 1915, Dent was asked to serve in Egypt but could not for personal reasons and instead opted to work in France. Dent served at Race

---

87. Brittain, 2009.
88. Powell, 2016.

Course Hospital in Rouen, France. According to Dent, that time was "[20] strenuous and crowded months."

For those nurses who came later, it was quite an adjustment coming from the hospitals in England to the tented camp hospitals in France and on other battlefronts. Dent described the adaption of new nurses to life at the field hospital:

> The newcomer to a camp hospital finds matters very different to what she has been accustomed in England; no hot water, no taps, no sinks, no fires, no gas-stoves, a regular Hood's 'November' of negation…These drawbacks seem a little depressing and over-whelming at first, but the adaptable girl soon learns to overcome such minor difficulties.[89]

If willing to learn — like Dent herself was — newcomers soon adjusted to the routine of hospital: "The early morning's work consisted of making 20 beds, dusting [24] lockers, taking [24] temperatures, and tidying the wards."[90]

Sometimes the nurses had unique tasks like using mental math to figure out the proper ratios to make food: Camp housekeeping in France quickly proved itself to be quite an arithmetical affair. Thus if one decided on making scones, immediately there was a little arithmetic to be done in ratios and substitutions, with the home quantity as a basis."[91] The day-to-day tasks, however, were more menial, like making beds, or more upsetting, like comforting wounded soldiers who were moaning, "I'm dying, I'm dying, I'm dying."

---

89. Ibid.
90. Powell, 2016.
91. Ibid.

On July 1, 1916, the first day of the Battle of the Somme, the number of patients overwhelmed the hospital. The staff had been prepared, but not for an onslaught like what happened. Even so, everyone at the hospital pitched in and worked hard: "Everyone turned with enthusiasm to the task they had in hand. Whatever our hand found to do on that memorable day and the four following days, we did with all our might."[92] At the end of the days, though, the night came with,

> a vision of Hell, cruel flesh-agony, hideous writhings, broken moanings, a boy-child sitting up in bed gibbering and pulling off his head bandages, a young Colonial coughing up his last life-blood, a big, so lately strong man with ashen face and blue lips, lying quite still but for a little fluttering breathing…[93]

Like other nurses who served during the war, these images stayed with Dent long after the end of the Great War.

After the war, Dent became a journalist, but she sadly died in 1930 at the young age of 45 at the Marie Curie Cancer Hospital in London. In the years following, Marie Curie Cancer Hospital established the Olive Dent Ward, and Lady Plunkett of the hospital received funds from various individuals to name beds in the Olive Dent Ward.

Elsie Inglis: Scottish Doctor and Suffragist

Dr. Elsie Inglis is the epitome of a woman who would not take no for an answer. When the Great War broke out in 1914, Elsie Inglis, as a qualified doctor, wanted to open a hospital in Edinburgh and serve on the front-lines, but the War Office turned her down, gently telling her to "go home

---

92. Ibid.
93. Ibid.

and sit still."[94] That did not faze the 50-year-old who had been working with women and children in the poorest parts of Edinburgh. If she could not get the War Office to help, she would found some hospitals herself. Her project became known as the Scottish Women's Hospitals. Inglis began establishing hospitals in a variety of Allied countries, most famously in Serbia, to treat thousands of wounded men from the unforgiving trenches. As one of Inglis's descendents, Patricia Purdom, remarked in 2017, "I think [Inglis] is quite pioneering to show [women] were not the weak species, if you like. She and her nurses went through some atrocious conditions when they were serving out in Russia, Serbia and France."[95]

Elsie Inglis, founder of the Scottish Women's Hospitals

94. "Elsie Inglis to be commemorated for war achievements," 2017.
95. Ibid.

Inglis traveled quite a bit throughout her life. The seventh of nine children, Inglis was born in 1864 in north India and lived there for 11 years. She briefly lived in Tasmania for three years before her parents moved to Edinburgh, Scotland in 1878. Inglis's moves as a child prepared her to travel across Europe during World War I.

The first Scottish Women's Hospital field unit was formed in Kragujevac, Serbia in December 1914. Within months, the entire country faced a typhus epidemic, which had already taken the lives of four medical personnel from the Scottish Women's Hospitals in Serbia. Undeterred, Inglis traveled to Serbia to establish four hospitals specifically to treat typhus. During the first year of the war, roughly 600 British women, including 60 doctors, served with the Scottish Women's Hospitals in either Serbia or Macedonia.[96]

 Women's suffrage organizations raised an equivalent of almost $75 million to support Inglis' work with the Scottish Women's Hospitals during World War I.[97]

When the Austrian army invaded Serbia in the fall of 1915 and the Serbians began the "great retreat" — which would take the lives of roughly 200,000 men, women, and children — Inglis remained with her hospital, even though she knew it meant that she and about 80 women who stayed with her would become prisoners of war (POWs).[98] According to Inglis' biographer, the Germans soon tired of Inglis and her staff and sent them home after a couple months.[99]

---

96. Allcock and Young, 2000.
97. "Elsie Inglis to be commemorated for war achievements," 2017.
98. Brocklehurst, 2017.
99. "Elsie Inglis to be commemorated for war achievements," 2017.

Near the end of 1916, even though Inglis had just learned she had cancer, she still traveled with the Serbs toward the Russian front and established two field hospitals staffed by 80 women.[100] Refusing to go home to England until the Serbs had received safe passage, Inglis arrived in Newcastle, England very frail. Transported to a nearby hotel, Inglis died on November 26, 1917.

Inglis's willingness to remain in Serbia when the country was devastated not only by invasion but also by a typhus epidemic, which killed about 16 percent of the population, ingratiated her to the Serbs.[101] In 2015, they honored Inglis and five other female volunteers with commemorative Serbian stamps. There is a famous saying in Serbia: "In Scotland they made her a doctor, in Serbia we would have made her a saint."[102]

After her death, Inglis was well respected in England. According to Arthur Balfour, Secretary of State for Foreign Affairs, "In the history of this World War, alike by what she did and by heroism, driving power and the simplicity with which she did it, Elsie Inglis has earned an everlasting place of honour."[103] Other countries felt even more strongly about Inglis's service during the war; Inglis posthumously received the highest awards in Russia and Serbia — the Gold St George Medal and White Eagle with Swords — which had never previously been awarded to a woman.[104]

Soldiers: The Daring Heroes

Given the traditional roles that women held in society in the early 20th century, it is no surprise that very few women served as soldiers. Winston

100. Brocklehurst, 2017.
101. "Elsie Inglis to be commemorated for war achievements," 2017.
102. Allcock and Young, 2000.
103. Hartley, 2003.
104. Ibid.

Churchill's words, although directed toward the Royal Air Force pilots during World War II, seem apt regarding women who served as soldiers in World War I: "Never in the field of human conflict was so much owed by so many to so few." The exact number of women who served on the front is unknown, as often women disguised themselves as men in order to join the troops. Western European nations in particular, such as England, France, and Germany, forbade women to fight and made them leave if they were discovered. Eastern European nations were slightly more lenient, as Austria-Hungary and Serbia allowed some women to serve openly, including the highly decorated Milunka Savić, a Serbian female combatant.[105]

For both World War I and World War II, the nation that was most open to women combatants was Russia. Roughly 1,000 Russian women fought during World War I, even before the provisional government tried to recruit them.[106] As the war grew increasingly unpopular in Russia and — along with food shortages and a disconnect from the people — brought about the abdication of Tsar Nicholas II, the new provisional government thought that an insurgence of women into the Russian Army might be able to bring new life into the demoralized Russian military. Maria Bochkareva, a non-commissioned officer with three years of combat experience, had championed this effort, successfully convincing Alexander Kerenskii, Supreme Commander of the Russian Army to authorize the formation of the Women's Battalion of Death in Petrograd near the end of May 1917. Placed in charge of the unit, Bochkareva issued a call to arms on May 21, 1917:

> Our mother is perishing. Our mother is Russia. I want to help save her. I want women whose hearts are pure, whose impulses are lofty.

---

105. Atwood, 2016.
106. Ibid.

With such women setting an example of self sacrifice, you men will realize your duty in this grave hour.[107]

The combination of the speech and its publication in the newspaper enticed 2,000 women to volunteer, although Bochkareva found only 300 women worthy to serve.[108]

Throughout the summer, several units based in other cities — another in Petrograd and new units in Moscow, Ekaterindor, Kiev, and Saratov — joined this first battalion.[109] By the fall of 1917, there were nearly 5,000 Russian female soldiers.[110] Some estimates even suggest that there were up to 50,000 women in the all-female battalions.[111] Unfortunately, however, the all-female units did not achieve the effect that Kerenskii and government leaders had intended: they did not goad the men to fight any stronger. Thus, beginning in the fall of 1917, the Russian provisional government no longer supported the units but continued to allow their existence. When the Bolsheviks gained control of the government in October 1917, the women's units began to disband. By early 1918, all the battalions of females had disintegrated.[112]

 One of the Women's Battalion of Death regiments in Petrograd — not Bochkareva's more famous battalion, which was on the front line fighting — helped defend the Winter Palace against the Bolsheviks during the October Revolution of 1917. Apparently, according to Major General Sir Alfred Knox, the British attaché (a diplomat who often has a special area of focus, such as the military) in Petrograd noted that the

107. Harris, 2017.
108. Ibid.
109. Noonan, 2001.
110. Beatty, 1918.
111. Pasvolsky, 1918.
112. Noonan, 2001.

Bolsheviks believed "the company of women offered the most serious resistance."[113]

Like Russia, the United States made an unprecedented decision and allowed women to serve as Navy yeomen — a petty officer who performed clerical duties — during the war. Even before the United States entered the war on April 6, 1917, the United States had already been considering allowing military involvement for women. In the spring of 1917, U.S. Secretary of the Navy Josephus Daniels posed a question to his counsel: "Is there any regulation which specifies that a Navy yeoman be man?" When it was clear that the Naval Act of 1916 called for "persons" and not men, Daniels extended the opportunity of becoming a yeoman to American women. On March 21, 1917, Loretta Walsh became the first woman Navy petty officer when sworn in as chief yeoman. For the next year and a half, until the end of the war in November 1918, 11,000 women joined the Navy as yeomen. They did not go overseas, but instead served stateside, often completing clerical work. Even so, they received the same benefits as male yeomen, including the same pay of $28.75 per month, and were honored as veterans after the war. When the war ended in late 1918, the Navy demobilized the women and became an all-male force again.

 Although the popular term for female yeomen was "yeomanettes," Secretary of the Navy Daniels rejected this appellation. According to him, "I never did like this 'ette' business. I always thought if a woman does a job, she ought to have the name of the job."[114] Thus, the Navy settled for calling men and women yeomen, but included a parenthetical "F" for female when assigning sea duty.[115]

The United States Marine Corps also allowed women to join but not until August 1918, and the Marines were very particular in their selection. For

---

113. Knox, 1921.
114. Gavin, 2006.
115. Ibid.

the four months until the end of the war, 305 women joined the Marines, including Opha Mae Johnson, who joined on August 13, 1918 and is thought to be the first female Marine.[116]

Maria Bochkareva: Founder of the Women's Battalion of Death

Maria Bochkareva was the Joan of Arc of World War I. In the introduction to her biography, Isaac Levine, Bochkareva's editor and assistan, noted how a correspondent in July 1917 had referred to Bochkareva as Joan of Arc and then expanded on the analogy:

> Indeed, in the annals of history since the days of the Maid of Orleans we encounter no feminine figure equal to Botchkareva [another spelling of her name]. Like Joan of Arc, this Russian peasant girl dedicated her life to her country's cause. If Botchkareva failed — and this is yet problematical, for who will dare forecast the future of Russia? — it would not lessen her greatness…Like Joan of Arc, Botchkareva is the symbol of her country.[117]

While Joan of Arc and Bochkareva were both born as peasant women, they differed in that Joan of Arc was single and died at 19 years of age while Bochkareva followed her husband to war and continued to fight even after her husband was killed. Both women also petitioned kings — Charles VII for Joan of Arc and Tsar Nicholas II for Bochkareva — to serve in their respective conflicts. Finally, both women were killed after difficulties with the leaders in their respective countries — Joan of Arc was burned at the stake for heresy while Bochkareva was executed by the Bolsheviks.

---

116. Ibid.
117. Bochkareva and Levine, 1919.

Maria Bochkareva

Born to a peasant family, Bochkareva had always been a strong woman. Originally rejected from fighting in combat because she was a woman, Bochkareva wrote a letter to the tsar himself, who granted her permission to join the war as a combatant. Wounded six times in battle and the recipient of the Cross of St. George several times, Bochkareva became a non-commissioned officer in the Russian army.[118] She later became the leader of the Russian Amazons, the Women's Battalion of Death, created to shame the Russian men into fighting after the abdication of the tsar. Although use for the all-female battalions died out when the Bolsheviks began to gain power in October 1917, Bochkareva was a recognized Russian and international hero for women. Almost everyone had heard of the Women's Battalion of

---

118. Pasvolsky, 1918.

Death. Unfortunately, Bochkareva's refusal to support the Bolsheviks cost Bochkareva her life. She briefly escaped to the United States after a Bolshevik attempt to execute her and dictated her life-story to Russian writer Isaac Don Levine. When Bochkareva returned to Russia, the Bolsheviks swiftly arrested and tried her. Bochkareva was executed on May 16, 1920.

Although certainly a woman worth studying for her own fighting abilities, Bochkareva was also a notable inspiration for all kinds of Russian women. As the February 1918 edition of The Red Cross Magazine noted, Bochkareva's Battalion of Death attracted Russian women of all types. Through her service and her battalion, Bochkareva popularized the idea of women combatants in World War I:

> Women of all stations in life have joined Maria Bochkareva's legion. There are peasant women, soldiers' widows, the daughters of generals and of rich men, college and university students who consider it now just as dignified for a woman to don a soldier's uniform as to wear the insignia of a Red Cross nurse.[119]

Bochkareva and the women in the Battalion of Death were known for their fierceness and their willingness to fight when the Russian men refused to do so, including even covering the retreat of some male troops.[120] The women trained just like the men, rising at 5 a.m. and drilling until 9 p.m., eating simple food and sleeping on bare boards, but in some instances, they seemed to exceed the men in bravery.[121] This is understandable: the women had more to prove, and the men were tired of fighting a futile war that they blamed on the tsar. Ultimately, the Bolshevik takeover of the Russian government in October 1917 brought an end to the Women's Battalion of

119. Ibid.
120. Ibid.
121. Ibid.

Death, but Bochkareva and her women would serve as examples in perpetuity of women who were willing to fight on the frontlines.

Maria Bochkareva and the Women's Battalion of Death

In August 1917, British nurse Florence Farmborough, who served with the First Flying Column, which followed the Eighth Army to Romania, learned of the Women's Death Battalion from a newspaper report. Farmborough's initial thoughts seemed fairly positive:

> Many of [the women], painted and powdered, had joined the Battalion as an exciting and romantic adventure; [Bochkareva] loudly condemned their behaviour and demanded iron discipline. Gradually the patriotic enthusiasm had spent itself; the 2,000 slowly dwindled to 250. In honour of these women volunteers, it was recorded that they *did* go into the attack; they *did* go 'over the top.'[122]

---

122. Powell, 2016.

But Farmborough did question the effectiveness of the battalion, as not all went 'over the top':

> Some remained in the trenches, fainting and hysterical; others ran or crawled back to the rear. Bachkarova [variation of Bochkareva] retreated with her decimated battalion; she was wrathful, heartbroken, but she had learnt a great truth: women were quite unfit to be soldiers.[123]

Farmborough's encounter with a woman soldier who did not belong to the Women's Death Battalion seemed to suggest that while some women like Bochkareva might be brilliant examples of women combatants, the vast majority of the women were not: "A woman soldier with a badly contused leg came to us for a dressing. She did not belong to the Women's Death Battalion; she had, however, heard of them and from her curt remarks one could understand that she held them in but little respect ..."[124]

Nonetheless, no matter what opinion people had of the Women's Death Battalion, Bochkareva accomplished an amazing feat: the woman who was only educated enough to scribble her name had trained thousands of women to fight alongside the boys.[125]

 The doughnut became popular thanks to some Salvation Army volunteers in World War I. In September 1917, four women located just outside the trenches in France began collecting materials to make doughnuts like back home in the States, but they had to improvise some. They used excess rations for dough; shell casings and wine bottles for rolling pins; and soldiers' helmets for frying the cruller doughnuts. The 250 volunteers of the Salvation Army became instantly popular with the soldiers, especially the Donut Lassies. One soldier wrote,

123. Ibid.
124. Ibid.
125. Bochkareva and Levine, 1919.

"Can you image hot doughnuts, and pie and all that sort of stuff? Served by might good looking girls, too."[126] Even though the Donut Lassies weren't fighting, they still got very close to the action. One woman, Stella Young, was saved by having stepped away from the stove just as a piece of shrapnel flew in the tent and cut through a donut pan.[127] If you want to make doughnuts like the Donut Lassies of World War I did, just search the Original World War I Donut Recipe by the Salvation Army on the internet search engine of your choice!

Flora Sandes: The Only British Woman who Officially Served as a Soldier in World War I

Growing up, Flora Sandes, born in 1876, had always wanted to be a part of the British cavalry who charged against the Russians at the Battle of Balaklava during the Crimean War, embodied by Alfred, Lord Tennyson's poem, "The Charge of the Light Brigade." In fact, Sandes even practiced shooting rabbits from horseback as a young woman in hopes of one day living out this dream.[128]

When war broke out between Britain, Russia, and Serbia against Germany, Austria-Hungary, and the Ottoman Empire, Sandes was 38 years old and living in London with her aging father. Her first attempts to get involved in the great worldwide conflict failed, however. She applied to be a part of a Voluntary Aid Detachment (VAD) but was turned down due to her connection to the women's suffrage movement and a claim the war would "only last six months."[129]

Sandes remained undeterred. A few days later, Sandes came into contact with Mabel Grouitch, the American wife of a Serbian official, who had come to England to recruit a medical unit of doctors and nurses to serve

---

126. Boissoneault, 2017.
127. Boissoneault, 2017Ibid.
128. Atwood, 2016.
129. Miller, 2012.

in Serbia. Grouitch accepted Sandes' request to work for the Serbian Red Cross, and Sandes soon got to know the other 36 nurses on the team, becoming close friends with Emily Simmonds.

Flora Sandes in her Serbian Army uniform

Sandes and Simmonds first arrived in Serbia in August 1914 to serve at the First Reserve Military Hospital in Kragujevac and was there until her three-month contract was up. Like other medical personnel who nursed the Serbians noted, Sandes too observed that the Serbs were extremely resilient in the face of pain, and she respected them greatly for that characteristic.

Sandes went to England and Simmonds went to the United States to raise more funds for medical supplies to take back to Serbia.

When the two women returned to Serbia in February 1915, they learned that a typhus epidemic, which originated in Valjevo, had devastatingly spread throughout the country. Eager to take the newly acquired supplies to Valjevo, Sandes and Simmonds ignored the warning of Colonel Subotić, the vice-president of the Serbian Red Cross. Both women faithfully served the Serbs, even coming down with typhus themselves. Both recuperated due to excellent nursing from their orderlies.

With the cessation of the epidemic at the beginning of the summer of 1915, Sandes returned to England, but was quick to go back to Serbia when she heard of Austro-Hungarian, Bulgarian, and German attacks against Serbia in October 1915. Sandes planned to work in Valjevo again, but the Austrian occupation of the city made it impossible. Thus, Sandes joined a medical team attached to a Serbian army because it was the only way she could continue to work in Serbia and became friends with the regiment's commander, Colonel Milić.

When the Bulgarians pushed the Serbian regiment Sandes' team was attached to into an area without roads, the medical team could no longer follow in its ox wagons and Sandes asked to stay as a private in the Serbian army. Colonel Milić agreed and introduced her to the commandant of the whole division, General Miloš Vasić.

 The Serbian army was one of the few armies in the world that would accept female soldiers. In fact, General Vasić even suggested to Sandes that her presence would inspire and encourage his men.

Joining her fellow soldiers in a difficult retreat through Albania, Sandes soon became a beloved part of the regiment. Known as "Nashi Engleskinja" ("Our Englishwoman"), the men even called her "brother," a term that they used among themselves. The officers and enlisted men alike saw Sandes as a representative of England, a "pledge."[130]

When the Serbian army made the great retreat across Albania, fighting their way through, Sandes and the men of the Fourth Company arrived on the coast of Albania on December 31, 1915. Aided by Simmonds, Sandes quickly began relief efforts for the remaining Serbs, which prompted her promotion from private to sergeant.

As Sandes did throughout the war, she returned to England to write a short book about her experiences in the Serbian army in hopes of rallying English support for the Serbian cause. She then went back to Serbia to fight against the Bulgarians in the summer of 1916. During a charge up a hill, Sandes was severely wounded on her right side from a Bulgarian grenade. This event actually did more to inform the British public about the plight of the Serbs, as news quickly reached England that a British woman had been wounded while serving in the Serbian army.

Ever the traveler, Sandes went back to England to recuperate and then soon returned to the battlefield near the end of World War I to be a part of the Serbian advance that pushed the Austrians, Bulgarians, and Germans out of Serbia. In view of all that she did for Serbia, a special Serbian Act of Parliament in June 1919 honored Flora Sandes by making her the first woman to be commissioned in the Serbian Army, promoting her to captain.[131] Sandes received seven medals during her service.

Demobilized from the Serbian army in 1922, Sandes struggled to adjust to civilian life. As she stated in her autobiography published in 1927,

---

130. Bourke, 2011.
131. Ibid.

I cannot attempt to describe what it now felt like, trying to get accustomed to a woman's life and a woman's clothes again; and also to ordinary society after having lived entirely with men for so many years. Turning from a woman to a private soldier proved nothing compared with turning back from soldier to ordinary woman.[132]

Sandes married Yuri Yudenitch, a former officer of the Imperial Russian Army, in 1927. He had fled Russia during the civil war between the Whites (of which he was a part) and the Reds (the Bolshevik communists) and joined the Serbian army. Yudenitch had actually served as one of Sandes's sergeants and was 12 years her junior.

 FUN FACT When Sandes married Yudenitch, she was 51 years old, and he was 39.

During World War II, Sandes and her husband Yudenitch resided in Serbia, then part of Yugoslavia. They desired to serve after the Germans invaded in 1941, but the invasion was over before they could assist. Yudenitch died of natural causes that same year, and Sandes stayed in Yugoslavia until the end of the war, first in jail and later under what was effectively house arrest. After World War II, Sandes returned to England for the last time; she died at the age of 80 in Suffolk, England on November 24, 1956.

Ecaterina Teodoroiu: First Female Romanian Officer and Romanian Heroine Who Died Serving Her Country

Born into a family of farmers in 1894, Ecaterina Teodoroiu (born Cătălina Toderoiu) grew up in the village of Vădeni and planned to become a teacher when she graduated from the Girl's School in Bucharest. In the summer of 1916, however, Romania entered World War I on the side of the Allies, and

---

132. Sandes, 1927.

Teodoroiu's plans changed. Her brothers immediately joined the army, and she volunteered as a nurse close to the fighting near the Jiu River.

Second Lieutenant Ecaterina Teodoroiu

 Teodoroiu was so eager to teach future students about Romanian heritage that she intently studied history and even joined a local scout troop to learn more about Romanian patriotism. In fact, she became part of the first female Romanian scout troop in Bucharest.[133]

Like Flora Sandes, Teodoroiu gradually moved toward serving in the Romanian army. First, along with some other scouts, Teodoroiu successfully

---

133. Atwood, 2016.

stopped the Germans from crossing the bridge over the Jiu River. Second, Teodoroiu continued to insist upon serving as a nurse as close as possible to the front lines and was commended for her efforts. Finally, upon the death of her brother Ion in battle, Teodoroiu decided to fight alongside her remaining brother, Nicolae, a sergeant-instructor.

Although not officially a part of the 18th Infantry Regiment, all the men accepted Teodoroiu as one of them. When a shell fell near Nicolae and killed him, Teodoroiu asked for permission to serve in his place. Although Romanian women were not normally allowed to serve in the military, the officers made an exception for Teodoroiu and allowed her to fight.

Teodoroiu's bravery during a skirmish with the Germans on November 4, 1916 won her the respect of many. The Germans had outnumbered and surrounded part of Teodoroiu's regiment. Speaking in German, Teodoroiu officially stated to the Germans that the Romanian regiment had decided to surrender and then began shooting, killing several Germans and allowing most of the company to escape. Teodoroiu and several other unfortunate soldiers were taken captive, but Teodoroiu took advantage of an inattentive German soldier and shot him, allowing the other Romanian soldiers and herself to escape. Even so, the Germans shot at the escaping Romanians in the darkness and wounded Teodoroiu in the right leg.

Teodoroiu refused to let this wound hinder her involvement, and she returned to the company that same evening. An exploding shell that wounded her in both legs some time later would force Teodoroiu to rest and recover in the hospital. During her recuperation, Teodoroiu was promoted to second lieutenant and became the first female officer in the Romanian army.

Teodoroiu recovered from her wounds in several months and was discharged from the hospital in January 1917. On March 10, 1917, she was awarded the Military Virtue Medal, 2nd Class for her courage in battle. A week later, Teodoroiu was awarded the Military Virtue Medal, 1st Class and given command of a 25-man platoon in the 7th Company, which was a new regiment for Teodoroiu. As the Romanian army went through a period of reorganization, Teodoroiu aspired to be an excellent commander of her platoon and, like the men, was eager to get out and fight again.

One commander asked Teodoroiu if she had enough provisions in the bag she was carrying. She swiftly replied that she did, but it was not for her. Rather, it was for the Germans. Opening up her bag, Teodoroiu revealed a bag full of bullets.[134]

Although encouraged to stay back and tend the wounded, Teodoroiu begged to go to the frontlines, and the division commander relented. As a group of Romanian units attempted to take an area near the German line, Teodoroiu's unit was slightly ahead, as her unit had advanced more quickly. Unfazed by the enemy, Teodoroiu led the charge from the front, goading her men to follow her. Within seconds, she was wounded in the chest and died almost immediately on September 3, 1917. Soldiers spread the news to one another: "The second lieutenant girl has died!"[135] After the war, Teodoroiu posthumously became a national hero because she had died serving the cause of Romania.

Initially buried close to the front near where she had fallen, Teodoroiu's remains were exhumed and interred in a crypt near the city center of Târgu Jiu. Teodoroiu would forever remain a national hero as the first Romanian woman to become a lieutenant and as a heroine who died in service to her country.

 Just as Maria Bochkareva was known as the Russian Joan of Arc, Romanians consider Ecaterina Teodoroiu their Joan of Arc. Even French General Henri Berthelot

134. Ibid.
135. Ibid.

of World War I considered Teodoroiu the Jeanne d'Arc of Romania due to her bravery and patriotism.[136]

Armistice Day, November 11, 1918, was the end of WWI. November 11 would come to be celebrated as Veterans Day every year in the United States.

---

136. Stroe, 2017.

Part II
World War II

The second great conflict of the 20th century, World War II, was a direct result of the Great War. Unlike World War I, where the actions of a variety of countries led to the worldwide conflict, one person brought about the Second World War: Adolf Hitler. Determined to avenge the Germans and the severe reparations required in the Treaty of Versailles, Hitler rose to power by championing a new hope for Germany.

At first, Germany was supported by the other Axis powers — Japan, the Soviet Union, and Italy, — but the latter two switched sides in the middle of the war. The Soviet Union signed a secret pact allying itself with Nazi Germany on August 23, 1939, which would stay in effect until Germany invaded the Soviet Union on June 22, 1941 and the U.S.S.R. joined the Allies. Likewise, Italy switched sides in 1943: it surrendered to the Allies on September 13, 1943, and one month later on October 13, 1943, it declared war on Nazi Germany.

The "Big Three" Allied nations were the United Kingdom under Winston Churchill, the United States under Franklin Delano Roosevelt, and the Soviet Union under Josef Stalin. The United Kingdom joined the war first in September 1939, with both the United States and the Soviet Union following in 1941. Other Allied nations included China, the colonies of the British Empire, and countries in Central and South America. The "Big Three," together with China were referred to as the "Big Four" and later became the "Four Policemen" in the United Nations.

1939 to 1945 are the commonly accepted dates for World War II. Even so, it is difficult to give an exact date for the beginning of the war. Did it occur on September 1, 1939 when Nazi Germany invaded Poland? Or did it start on September 29, 1938 when Germany, Italy, Great Britain, and France signed the Munich agreement, which forced Czechoslovakia to cede the Sudetenland with key military defense positions to Nazi Germany? Or perhaps even earlier when Germany incorporated Austria in the Anschluss in March 1938? Yet, these are only dates that occurred in Europe. In some respects, one could say that World War II began on September 18, 1931 when Japan invaded Manchuria or on July 7, 1937 when Japan invaded China. In any case, by the end of December 1941 after the attack on Pearl Harbor, most major (and many minor) countries around the world found themselves involved in World War II.

After the invasion of Poland in 1939, Great Britain and France both declared war on Nazi Germany, but they took little action against the other country. By 1940, Germany had control of Belgium, Denmark, France, the Netherlands, and Norway. Under German occupation, France could do little to aid Britain in its fight against Nazi Germany. On May 10, 1940, Winston Churchill replaced the appeaser Nelville Chamberlain as Prime Minister and vowed that Britain would not be defeated by Germany without a fight. He oversaw the evacuation of over 300,000 stranded soldiers from Dunkirk, France from May 26 to June 4, 1940. Although officially a German tactical victory, the success at Dunkirk was a significant morale booster for the British people, and it gave the country the drive it needed to take on the extremely powerful Nazi Germany.

Under Roosevelt, the United States initiated the first peacetime draft in 1940, but most Americans did not wish to go to war. Instead, the Lend-Lease Act was passed in March 1941 to allow the United States to transfer arms and military aid to foreign nations, especially to England, without full involvement in World War II. The American position quickly changed with the surprise attack on Pearl Harbor on December 7, 1941, which resulted in the deaths of over 2,000 Americans.

As Hitler and the Nazis initiated their plan to exterminate Jews in 1942, in what we now know as the Holocaust, the United States was engaged in many campaigns and naval battles in the Pacific against the Japanese. The United States was also fighting with the Allies against the Axis units in North Africa.

1942 and 1943 brought what we would consider today significant turning points of the war. When the United States defeated Japan in the Battle of Midway in June 1942, it was considered a decisive moment in the Pacific theater. When the Soviet Union defeated the Germans at Stalingrad, Germany would advance no farther in Eastern Europe and began to be pushed back by the Soviets. Beginning on January 5, 1943, the Tunisian campaign in North Africa led to the capitulation of the Axis troops on May 13, 1943.

But of course, the most famous turning point occurred on June 6, 1944 (D-Day) with the Allied landings on the Normandy beaches. On this day alone, over 4,000 Allied men died.[137] The success of the Battle of Normandy allowed the Allies to push through France, forcing the Germans to retreat back into Germany. As a last-ditch effort, the Germans advanced 50 miles into Allied lines during their last offensive, which became known as the Battle of the Bulge. With the German defeat on January 16, 1945, the Allies began the push into Germany, crossing the Rhine on March 22,

---

137. "D-Day Landings," 2016.

1945. As American, British, and Soviet troops spread throughout Germany with consecutive German defeats, the Third Reich began to crumble. The Soviet Red Army was the first to reach Berlin, and Germany surrendered on May 7, 1945, shortly after Hitler and his wife, Eva Braun, committed suicide on April 30, 1945.

The Japanese, however, had not given up. The Soviets promised to enter the war against the Japanese three months after the German surrender, which occurred on May 8 for them, but it turned out they had no need to do so. On July 16, 1945, the United States conducted the first successful test of the atomic bomb. Based on the recovery of a codebook on Okinawa in June 1945, American codebreakers learned how extensive the Japanese preparations were on their home island. It was estimated that Allied forces could expect up to 1 million casualties if they attempted landings in Japan.

Given these facts, President Harry S. Truman, who became president after Roosevelt's death on April 12, 1945, decided that he did not want to waste the lives of any more American men. After careful consultation, top American military officials decided upon four cities that had more military significance rather than cultural significance. On August 6, 1945, the Enola Gay, a B-29 Superfortress, dropped an atomic bomb known as "Little Boy" on Hiroshima. Three days later, on August 9, another atomic bomb was dropped on Nagasaki. On August 14, 1945, Japan signed a surrender agreement on the U.S.S. Missouri in Tokyo Bay on September 2, 1945. World War II was finally over.

Over 60 million people, more than half of whom were civilians, were killed during World War II, making it not only the most geographically widespread conflict but also the deadliest conflict in history. At one point, 230 million Europeans fell under Nazi rule.[138] By the end of 1943, Germany

---

138. Manning, 2014.

faced a war on three sides: the Mediterranean Front, spread across Africa and southern Europe, was almost 3,000 kilometers long; the Eastern Front through Russia spread 2,000 kilometers; and the Western Front in Europe spanned 6,000 kilometers.[139]

"Little Boy" atomic bomb, before being loaded into
Enola Gay's bomb bay

Even though Germany had all this territory to defend, the Soviet Union suffered the most casualties, over 21 million, and the Eastern Front was the bloodiest theater of the war. In fact, most of the German casualties were on the Eastern Front. Many historians even believe that the Battle of Stalingrad was the bloodiest battle not only in World War II but also throughout the entire course of history.

---

139. Ibid.

Famous Battles	Dates of the Battles	Interesting Facts about the Battles
Invasion of Poland	September 1-October 6, 1939	Both Germany and the Soviet Union invaded Poland based on the secret Nazi-Soviet Pact of August 1939, which stated that Poland would be partitioned between the two powers.
Battle of Sedan	May 12-15, 1940	The success of the German Blitzkreig ("lightning war") during this battle effectively removed France from the war.
Battle of Britain	July 10-October 31, 1940	The Air Battle for England gets its name from Winston Churchill's speech to the House of Commons on June 18, 1940: "What General Weygand has called The Battle of France is over. The Battle of Britain is about to begin."

Famous Battles	Dates of the Battles	Interesting Facts about the Battles
Invasion of Soviet Union	June 22-December 5, 1941	The German invasion so surprised Stalin that at first, he told the Soviet army not to respond. It would be hours later at noon that he would tell them to resist. He also did not address the Soviet Union publicly until 11 days after the attack.
Attack on Pearl Harbor	December 7, 1941	Over 2,000 Americans were killed during this 90-minute surprise attack by the Japanese. It was a "day of infamy," as President Franklin Delano Roosevelt stated.
Battle of the Coral Sea	May 4-8, 1942	This was the first battle in which aircraft carriers engaged each other.
Battle of Midway	June 4-7, 1942	Thanks to American codebreakers, including some females, the U.S. Navy knew ahead of time of the date and location of the planned attack, greatly contributing to the ultimate U.S. victory.

Famous Battles	Dates of the Battles	Interesting Facts about the Battles
Battle of Stalingrad	August 23, 1942- February 2, 1943	Often regarded as the single largest (nearly 2.2 million personnel) and bloodiest (1.8-2 million captured, wounded, or killed), the Battle of Stalingrad is often seen as the war's turning point because the Germans did not make any further advances in the U.S.S.R.
Battle of El Alamein	October 23- November 11, 1942	This battle was the first major Allied success against the Axis.
Battle of Normandy	June 6-August 30, 1944	The surprise invasion on June 6 (D-Day) and the success of the Normandy campaign allowed for the rapid liberation of western Europe.
Battle of Leyte Gulf	October 23-26, 1944	Considered the largest naval battle in World War II and potentially in history, this battle effectively crippled Japanese naval capabilities.

Famous Battles	Dates of the Battles	Interesting Facts about the Battles
Battle of the Bulge	December 16, 1944-January 25, 1945	The name "Battle of the Bulge" was coined by the press to describe the bulge in the German front lines on maps, and it was the last major German offensive campaign on the Western Front.
Battle of Luzon	January 9-August 15, 1945	General Douglas MacArthur wanted to liberate the Philippines from Japanese occupation, and Luzon was the largest of the Philippine islands. The author's grandfather also personally fought in this battle.
Battle of Iwo Jima	February 19-March 26, 1945	Joe Rosenthal's Associated Press photo of the raising of the American flag on the top of Mount Suribachi by six U.S. Marines was the iconic image of the battle itself and the war in the Pacific.
Battle of Berlin	April 16-May 2, 1945	Some German units fought westward to surrender to the Western Allies rather than to the Soviet Union.

The U.S. Marine Corps War Memorial in Washington, D.C., known as the
"Iwo Jima Monument."

I. Home Front

Chapter 4

Mothers, Daughters, and Wives

"Soldiers on the Home Front"

Like the women who stayed at home during World War I and supported their fathers, sons, and husbands from the Home Front, the women who remained at home during World War II did what they could to help the effort.

However, there were more opportunities available to women during the Second World War, likely due to the increased awareness about women's rights that had occurred after the First World War. At the very minimum, even if an American woman did not contribute in any other way, she almost always had a Victory Garden and made do with less, especially given that many items were rationed. As Betty Crocker noted in her cookbook:

> Hail to the women of America! You have taken up your heritage from the brave women of the past. Just as did the women of other wars, you have taken your positions as soldiers on the Home Front. . . . So to you women behind the men, behind the guns, we offer this little book, with its daily helps for wartime mealplanning and cooking.[140]

---

140. Crocker, 1943.

YOUR VICTORY GARDEN
counts more than ever!

A World War II poster promoting Victory Gardens

These women are often unnamed, but they are the unsung heroes of World War II. They quietly supported their men by running their households, not spending money on frivolous items, and taking the time to write countless letters to their loved ones overseas, some of whom they wouldn't see for two years or more. Because many of these women grew up in the Great Depression that had devastated America in the 1930s, it came naturally to them.

FUN FACT The 1940s had its own version of email! Letters could sometimes be expensive to write and mail, and the men overseas often didn't have the time to write a long letter. The solution was V-Mail, or Victory Mail. Service members and family members would write short notes on special pieces of paper, which were then microfilmed to transport overseas and reproduced at one-quarter of the original size for the recipient.

Even so, letters were still more popular, with V-Mail only representing 12 percent of the mail sailors received in 1944.[141]

My Grandma Basinger was one of these women. She married my grandfather on October 8, 1944, right before my grandfather shipped off to join the 158th Bushmasters Army unit that was headed to the Philippines. She accompanied him to some training, got some experience babysitting (as my grandfather remembered in his memories about the war), and wrote him countless letters during the years they were separated.

The author's Grandma and Grandpa Basinger in 1944.

Some women, especially those who were single, wanted to even go a step further and contribute more to the war effort. These women served as land girls on farms or as industrial workers in factories in the cities. One symbol of the women who worked as industrial workers lives on to this day — Rosie the Riveter — and continues to represent the power of the American woman.

141. "V-Mail."

Land Girls: The Rural Heroes

After the Industrial Revolution gained traction in America during the 1800s, the percentage of American workers who were farmers started to decrease. Even so, at 18.8 percent of the labor force, farmers still represented almost one-fifth of American workers.[142] As American men began to head off to war after Pearl Harbor in December 1941, the farming community started to see a labor shortage in 1942. Of course, the women became the new labor force.

At first, women joined the farming community informally. Farmers' wives and daughters who had always helped out around the farm started to take primary direction of the farms. The officially reported workforce of female farmers rose from not even 1 percent before World War II started to 13 percent within the first year of the war.[143]

From 1917 to 1919, the United States also had a Women's Land Army during World War I. Called the Women's Land Army of America, the women who worked on the farms were known as farmerettes.

As more and more men were sent overseas, the United States government knew that it needed a more formal solution and created the Women's Land Army in 1943, which became a quasi-military civilian group. Modeled after the Women's Land Army in Great Britain, the U.S. Women's Land Army trained women who lived in the cities and suburbs how to work on a farm. They, too, could wear uniforms if they purchased the optional official Women's Land Army uniforms.

The Women's Land Army in Great Britain had a variety of jobs for women: every land girl did some

---

142. Lebergott, 1966.
143. Yellin, 2004.

sort of dairy work; some land girls caught rats while others were a part of the Timber Cops and were called "Timber Jills"; and occasionally land girls worked alongside POWs.[144] There were also strict rules about how to wear the uniform coat, just like in the military.

Given the option of a variety of different schedules, from just working a couple weeks in the summer to working the entire summer to even relocating from the city to a farm more permanently, American women from towns and cities became farm workers under the Women's Land Army. The United States Department of Agriculture Extension Service estimated that it placed 1.5 million nonfarm women in farm jobs through the Land Army between 1943 and 1945 and that the same number of women found work on their own.[145]

Calling themselves "soldiers in overalls," the women who served in the U.S. Women's Land Army saw their jobs just as significant as women who joined the WACs or WAVES, the women's branches of the military. And it's true.[146] Without the work of the Women's Land Army, food would have been extremely scarce at home and overseas. While the Women's Land Army is one of the least known aspects of World War II, it is one that we should not neglect in our discussion.

A North Carolina farmer and the father of one American woman who served in the Land Army, noted, "Men may have fought to defend the land but women toiled it. Women saved our heritage."[147]

---

144. Mason, 2018.
145. Litoff and Smith, 1993.
146. Ibid.
147. Ibid.

Industrial Workers: The Urban Heroes

Thanks to the iconic Rosie the Riveter, the urban counterparts of the American land girls were much more popular. As men left to serve overseas, women chipped in on farms and in cities. Roughly 12 million women served during the war as industrial workers in places from foundries and warehouses to shipyards and steel mills.[148] They were welders, manufacturers, and, yes, even riveters. The majority of women worked in the aircraft industry, growing from just 1 percent of the industry's total workforce to 65 percent in 1943.[149]

After Pearl Harbor, President Franklin Roosevelt called for Americans to out-produce their enemies overwhelmingly. Just a few more planes, tanks, guns, and ships were not sufficient. American industry needed to do more. Largely due to American women, the United States was able to meet the military production goals that Roosevelt set.

Because the United States did not experience the devastating bombings that Great Britain and other Europeans had — and likely due to America's can-do attitude to out-work and out-produce the enemy — American industry provided almost two-thirds of all the Allied military equipment produced during the war: 297,000 aircraft, two million army trucks, 193,000 artillery pieces, and 86,000 tanks.[150]

The United States quickly became the military production powerhouse for the Allies. For example, the automobile industry completely changed to defense work only. In 1941, the United States automobile industry man-

---

148. Graves.
149. "Rosie the Riveter," 2010.
150. "War Production," 2007.

ufactured over 3 million cars, but from 1942 to 1945, only 139 cars were manufactured.[151]

 FUN FACT The United States built more planes in the year 1944 alone than Japan did from 1939 to 1945.[152]

As a side benefit, those 12 million women made more money than they had ever earned before. For many, it was their first time working outside of the home and their first time earning a paycheck. Although many women would return to the traditional role as homemaker when the war ended, some women enjoyed the newfound freedom and continued to work outside of the home.

Rosie the Riveter: The Iconic American Heroine

Now an iconic image for women, Rosie the Riveter was a fictional woman based on a female industrial worker. There is much debate about who the real Rosie actually was; suggestions include Geraldine Hoff Doyle, who is the traditionally accepted Rosie; Rose Will Monroe, who was featured in a promotional film for war bonds; and Naomi Parker Fraley, who was photographed in 1942 wearing a polka-dotted bandana, just like Rosie.[153]

No matter which woman inspired Rosie, she was the "every woman" of America's defense efforts, and she was crafted to recruit more female workers into defense industries. You can find Rosie's now recognizable red bandana all across America, making her perhaps the most successful recruitment tool in American history.

---

151. Ibid.
152. Ibid.
153. "Rosie the Riveter," 2010.

Women who served in defense industries during World War II called themselves Rosie the Riveters. And the women who worked as riveters didn't just wear the bandana to be cute — it kept them from getting their hair caught in the machine and their hair getting completely ripped out.

Anyone could recognize Norman Rockwell's depiction of Rosie with a flag in the background, stomping on Adolf Hitler's "Mein Kampf" in the May 29, 1943 Saturday Evening Post. In this illustration, Rosie looks pretty masculine.

The earlier version, however, was created by J. Howard Miller in 1942 and was featured on a poster for Westinghouse Electric Corporation under the headline, "We Can Do It!" This Rosie is much more feminine, although she still displays the iconic arm flex.

But no matter which version American women saw first, the depiction of a female industrial worker was powerful, and today those images of Rosie the Riveter serve as beacons for women's empowerment. As one United States government advertisement asked, "Can you use an electric mixer? If so, you can learn to operate a drill." Spurred on by Rosie, 12 million women did just that when they became workers in the defense industry.

Rosie the Riveter

Chapter 5

Actresses and the USO

"People Making Small Sacrifices for Victory"

Most women quietly helped the war effort from home, but for a few select women, they had more of a public effect. They were the actresses who boosted morale at home and abroad and the USO workers who brought a piece of American entertainment to those serving overseas.

Hollywood itself did what it could to contribute to the war effort. Most of the movies it produced during World War II emphasized patriotism and people coming from diverse ethnic backgrounds to fight for their wonderful country. In particular, many films included women playing a major and active role in the war effort. Women were depicted as welders, riveters, combat nurses, and even mothers and wives who supported their husbands from afar.[154]

Even with the government restricting the money that could be spent making films during the war years, Hollywood still enjoyed a nice profit. Perhaps as a way to get away from all the pain, worry, and stress, the American people attended the movies at near-record level of 90 million a week.[155]

---

154. Mintz and McNeil, 2018.
155. Ibid.

A government information manual came out about motion picture, urging directors to ask the question: "Will this picture help to win the war?"[156] Additionally, the manual encouraged directors to include images of "people making small sacrifices for victory — making them voluntarily, cheerfully, and because of the people's own sense of responsibility."[157]

In addition to its efforts on the screen, Hollywood actors and actresses also organized bond drives and set out containers for scrap metal and rubber. Some actresses like Betty Grable, Hedy Lamarr, Dorothy Lamour, and Lana Turner were extremely successful in selling war bonds, charging thousands of dollars for a kiss.[158]

Betty Grable

156. Ibid.
157. Ibid.
158. Yellin, 2004.

In a way, the few actresses who put up a good front for the war effort represented the millions of American women who were unknown but still did their part. Whether women helped by being good mothers or good actresses, every woman played a small part in helping to win the war.

Actresses: The Public Heroes

Due to their public recognition, actresses were great public faces for bond drives. In 1942, the Hollywood War Activities Committee and the Treasury Department decided to capitalize on the success of actresses raising money for the war effort. They organized a colossal tour of 337 actresses and actors called Stars Over America to raise money through war bonds.[159]

Names that seem unfamiliar to us now but that were quite common then joined the tour, including Bette Davis, Irene Dunne, Greer Garson, Paulette Goddard, Veronica Lake, Hedy Lamarr, Dorothy Lamour, Myrna Loy, Gene Tierney, and Jane Wyman.[160]

The 1942 tour, which started on the steps of the Treasury Department, visited over 300 cities and towns in one month and ended in New York City. It was a success, raising $775 million for the war effort.[161]

USO Workers: The Morale Heroes

Formed in February 1941, the United Service Organizations (USO) was a conglomeration of six civilian service organization — the YMCA, the YWCA, the National Catholic Community Service, the National Jewish

---

159. Yellin, 2004.
160. Ibid.
161. Ibid.

Welfare Board, the Travelers Aid Association, and the Salvation Army — that united to boost morale among the troops.[162]

There were USO-operated centers all across America and overseas, and they recruited female volunteers — also known as junior hostesses — to serve doughnuts, talk with the troops, and even dance with them. In October 1943, the USO extended its services and created an affiliate organization called Camp Shows, which would provide live entertainment from celebrities for the troops.

 Junior hostesses were not allowed to dance with other women when service members were present and could not refuse to dance with a serviceman unless he was dancing "conspicuously" or acting "ungentlemanly."

At first, the USO shows were just domestic, but they later expanded to overseas. While the shows didn't have a standard format, they included some mixture of actors and actresses, comedians, dancers, musicians, and singers. Many of the stars who went overseas were less well-known, except Bob Hope, who is widely remembered for his contributions.

Even so, occasionally big-name stars would tour overseas, including Kay Francis, Carole Landis, Mitzi Mayfair, and Martha Raye, who all turned a six-week tour of Europe and Africa into a five-month one. Landis recorded their memories into a book "Four Jills in a Jeep," which was later made into a film. The women experienced exactly what every man experienced on the front: an air raid.[163] Except the women did it in high heels.

Some stars made quite an impression on their audiences. Marlene Dietrich, German by birth but a nationalized American citizen, came to Europe to

---

162. Ibid.
163. Ibid.

tour and expressed her fears of going to German-held territory to General George S. Patton. The general urged her to keep on because the troops would know that they could get through it if Marlene Dietrich was risking her life there. And he gave her a revolver, which Dietrich said that she kept the entire war but never used.[164]

Four Jills in a Jeep movie poster

Years later, service member after service member would remember those performances fondly. It helped bring a little bit of America to the front and helped them forget about all the death and destruction. The 428,521 USO shows both at home and abroad featured over 7,000 performers, all of whom had done their job.[165]

164. Ibid.
165. Ibid.

Judy Garland: The Girl Next Door

Judy Garland, born Francis Ethel Gumm, was one of the more prominent women who worked with the USO. Because many GIs had grown up watching Garland as Dorothy in "The Wizard of Oz," they loved to watch her perform. It made them feel good about themselves and their country.

Garland served by physically attending a variety of USO performances stateside, including being one of the first to perform for the troops, starting in 1941, by using her recognizable voice on radio programs overseas and selling war bonds.[166] She even spent her honeymoon with Dave Rose on a USO tour.[167]

Garland loved the work, as she described in a 1942 Hollywood Report article:

> The immense thrill and gratification of doing what little I could to entertain came first. . . the friendships made with the boys and the knowledge that we can never do enough for the soldiers who have left their homes and families to fight our battles.[168]

Most women definitely would have shared Garland's sentiment of doing whatever they could to help the soldiers who had left their homes and families to fight overseas, but they didn't have the range of influence that Garland and others had as actresses. The encouraging aspect of American life was that each woman served in whatever position she found herself. The amazing wives and mothers who planted victory gardens and maintained their homes were just as involved in winning the war and supporting the soldiers as the more well-known actresses.

---

166. Quigley, 2015.
167. Rose, 2008.
168. Quigley, 2015.

While many accounts focus on the work of the everyday woman, USO workers and actresses like Judy Garland were integral to the war effort as the public face. Whether they were raising money for a bond drive or entertaining soldiers, sailors, and Marines at home and abroad, these women were the morale boosters of World War II.

Chapter 6

Journalists and Code-Breakers

*"Women Who Can Do a Man's Job
But Still Look like Women"*

While actresses and USO workers might have been the public front of the war effort that everyone could see, some largely unknown women made essential contributions to the well-being of the American public that were sometimes less obvious to the public. These women served as journalists and code-breakers.

Just like during World War I, journalism was an area not often open to women. However, with more men getting shipped off overseas, more opportunities arose for female journalists. The military alone had accredited 127 American female photographers and reporters to cover the war overseas by 1945.[169]

These women witnessed countless horrors as they wrote about and photographed the war overseas. For example, one of the most prolific and well-known female World War II photographers Margaret Bourke-White, who worked for Life magazine, photographed the Nazis bombing the Kremlin at night in 1941, her torpedoed ship when she boarded a lifeboat in De-

---

169. Yellin, 2004.

cember 1942, combat in Italy, air raids over Germany, and even Buchenwald, the first Nazi concentration camp that was liberated in 1945.[170]

FUN FACT INS (International News Service) journalist Lee Carson's report on the Malmedy Massacre, where German soldiers killed American POWs near Malmedy, Belgium, was one of the first accounts. Later, the site was photographed, and those pictures were used as evidence in the Nuremberg trials against the German officer in charge.[171]

Unlike journalists and photographers, code-breakers did not have the same visible impact on the public, but their actions directly contributed to the success of the war. It is only years after the war that we have become aware of all that women did in ending the war against the Nazis and the Japanese.

Journalists: The Investigative Heroes

In 1943, Newsweek ran an article in which it discussed the rising number of women who were serving in the Washington press corps. Unfortunately, the article didn't speak much about the talent of women. Instead, it noted that women still didn't have the same rights as men who were doing the same job and observed that the female journalists differed widely in appearance and in style of writing.

Rather than focus on the distinctions in writing, the article listed the physical differences of the women, including May Craig, Winifred Mallon, and Lee Carson. At the end, the article mentioned appearances yet one more time: "[female journalists are] women who can do a man's job but still look like women in not too severely tailored clothes and becoming hats."

---

170. Ibid.
171. Sorel, 2011.

Rebecca West: British Dame Turned Writer

At the end of the war, the Allied forces held a series of military tribunals to try prominent political and military leaders of Nazi Germany who had participated in the Holocaust and committed other war crimes. Held in Nuremberg, Germany, the Nuremberg War Crimes Trials were held between November 20, 1945 and October 1, 1946 and given the task of trying 24 leaders of the Third Reich.

Roughly 250 journalists crowded the courtroom on the opening day and verdict announcement day on August 31, 1946. One of these journalists was British Dame Cicely Isabel Fairfield, more commonly known as Rebecca West. Adopting her pseudonym from Henrik Ibsen's play "Rosmersholm," West was an author, journalist, and literary critic.

Well-known in England and America, she established her reputation as a spokeswoman for feminist and socialist causes and as a book critic. In 1948, when President Harry Truman presented her with the Women's Press Club Award for Journalism, he called her "the world's best reporter."

Harold Ross of The New Yorker assigned her to cover the trials in Nuremberg. Her account was later published into a book called "A Train of Powder" in 1955. The language of West's account is descriptive and captivating. She did not merely capture the words said, but she got at the emotions behind the trial. For example, West described Göring as someone who used imperial gestures, Schacht as stiff as a plank like a corpse, and Schirach as Jane Eyre.

She even captured the significance of the war trials in vibrant words: "Something is happening all over the world; one reads of it constantly in the newspapers, but here in Nuremberg one can feel it. A machine is running down . . . the war machine . . ."[172] The war trials were ushering in the end of an empire — the Third Reich — and the end of an era of war.

West ended her account in The New Yorker with some chilling words that encapsulated the atrocities of the Nazis and the readiness of all the Allies to begin a new life now that the menace of the Nazis was gone: "Before one of the eight judges could take his seat on the bench, some millions had to come to Europe. But now everybody wants to go home."[173]

Code-Breakers: The Mathematical Heroes

Many are familiar with Alan Turning and the British intelligence agency MI6's attempts to crack the Nazi code Engima from the 2014 movie "The Imitation Game." What you might not realize, however, is that countless American women helped break Nazi and Japanese codes.

Starting in the fall of 1941, some female students at the Seven Sisters college — Barnard College, Bryn Mawr College, Mount Holyoke College, Radcliffe College, Smith College, Vassar College, and Wellesley College — received mysterious letters inviting them to meet one-on-one with specific professors.

If the professor was convinced that a particular woman would be good at solving math and wasn't planning on getting married, she received a confidentiality agreement and started on-campus classes in code breaking. Pregnancy meant discharge, even for married women.

Recruited by and employed under the auspices of the U.S. Army and Navy after May 1942, many of the roughly 10,000 women codebreakers came

---

172. West, 1946.
173. Ibid.

from elite colleges. Later, however, the American government branched out and included women from a wider range of colleges and former schoolteachers.

These women worked in several different locations in the United States and held a variety of different jobs pertaining to code-breaking. Many women worked day in and day out, tediously trying to decipher a pattern in columns of numbers and letters or building "bombe" machines to try to decode German messages sent out through Enigma.

These women did amazing work in Europe and the Pacific. The United States was able to sink countless Japanese ships and occasionally was even able to stop attacks, all thanks to the work of these women. They also had some more enjoyable tasks, like creating phony coded American messages in the days leading up to Operation Overlord and the invasion of Normandy.

As in other professions, most of the female codebreakers were asked to leave and rejoin civilian life after the war. Even so, they were warned (as they had been during their time as codebreakers) not to speak about their service. A few women were allowed to continue as codebreakers, particularly Ann Caracristi who became the head of an Army research unit at the young age of 23.[174] She would later become the first female deputy director of the National Security Agency.

Although we often tend to view code-breaking as the work of a single genius like Turning, in reality, code-breaking during World War II was a large team effort where people shared different patterns, combinations, and ciphers to contribute to the greater cause. And over 10,000 women played a part.

---

174. Mundy, 2017.

II. Service

Chapter 7

Nurses and Red Cross Workers

"I Feel I am Doing a Real Worthwhile Thing"

Nursing has historically been considered a more feminine profession, and World War II was no exception. In fact, men were not allowed to serve as military nurses during the Second World War. Ironically, though, more than any other group of women, nurses and Red Cross workers came closest to the front.

More than 59,000 women served as Army nurses and 11,000 served as Navy nurses during the war. Of those 70,000, half of them — 35,000 — as well as 7,000 Red Cross girls served overseas.[175] Over 3.5 million women volunteered to assist with the Red Cross on the Home Front, including joining the Nurse's Aides and Gray Ladies divisions.[176]

For those who weren't quite ready to deal with the blood and guts of nursing, being a Red Cross girl who served overseas was a pretty good alternative. Operating clubmobiles, or traveling kitchens, in the European, Mediterranean, and North African theaters, Red Cross girls would serve coffee and deliver doughnuts to the troops. Because they followed the troops on major campaigns, they were the women who got closest to the front lines.

175. Yellin, 2004.
176. Ibid.

WWII Army Nurse Corps recruitment poster

Interestingly, the military services did not require a college degree if one en-listed, but the Red Cross did. You also had to be at least 25 years old to be a Red Cross girl.[177] The servicemen loved the Red Cross girls because they kept them company. They could show the Red Cross girls pictures of their girls back home, play games with them, drink coffee and eat doughnuts with them, and even dance with them.

Many of the letters that Red Cross girls sent home dealt with coffee, dough-nuts, or both. In one letter that she sent home, however, Gysella Simon, a Red Cross club director in England and Europe was more serious: "[M]ost of the time I feel I am doing a real worthwhile thing and it makes me glow

177. Ibid.

with satisfaction. I should like to share this feeling with every American girl back home."[178]

Nurses: The Caring Heroes

Formed in 1901 and 1908 respectively, the Army Nurse Corps and the Navy Nurse Corps had originally allowed women who joined to work as civilians serving with the military. In 1920, Army nurses received relative ranking with men while Navy nurses were not given relative ranking until 1944.[179]

Most of the nurses who served during World War II served on the Home Front, but 35,000 Army and Navy nurses served overseas. These women experienced the dangers of the front and witnessed the horrors of the concentration camps. Many even became POWs.

They were often right in the middle of the combat, including the first and only time during World War II when Army nurses landed with the invasion force during Operation Torch, the North African campaign. Sixteen women died during World War II as the direct result of enemy fire.[180]

 President Roosevelt proposed that nurses be drafted in his January 1945 State of the Union address. Congress wrote a bill, which passed the House and only needed one approval vote when Germany surrendered in May 1945.

---

178. Ibid.
179. Ibid.
180. Ibid.

Unlike the men who often had been drafted to serve, these 70,000 women volunteered as nurses. The day before her death on October 21, 1944 by German shell fire, Lieutenant Frances Y. Slanger penned a letter discussing her admiration for the men fighting and sent it to the military newspaper, Stars and Stripes.

The newspaper received countless replies to its publication of Slanger's letter, including one particularly poignant letter: "To all Army nurses overseas: We men were not given the choice of working in the battlefield or the home front. We cannot take any credit for being here. We are here because we have to be. You are here because you felt you were needed."[181]

Florence A. Blanchfield: "The Little Colonel"

Born in Shepherdstown, West Virginia, Florence A. Blanchfield was the fourth of eight children. During World War I, she enlisted as an Army nurse and was acting chief nurse in Angers, France and Coëtquidan, France from 1917 to 1919. She was 35 at the time.

After just a few short months as a civilian, Blanchfield returned to active duty in 1920, serving in the United States as well as overseas in Tianjin, China and in the Philippines. In 1935, Blanchfield joined the Office of the Army Surgeon General in Washington, D.C., becoming assistant superintendent in 1939, acting superintendent in 1942, and superintendent from June 1943 to September 1947.

Under Blanchfield, the number of Army nurses grew from 7,000 on December 7, 1941 to over 50,000 nurses by the end of the war.[182] Due to

---

181. Ibid.
182. Pierce, 2017.

her efforts on behalf of the Army nurses, Blanchfield received the Distinguished Service Medal in 1945.

One of Blanchfield's favorite stories to tell was about nurses who entered a town full of wounded men and ran out of supplies. But they were ready, and they improvised, tearing up government-issued underwear to make bandages.[183]

Blanchfield also played a major role in gaining full rank and benefits for nurses, culminating with the passage of the Army and Navy Nurse Corps Act of April 1947. Blanchfield herself became the first woman to receive a regular military commission in the Army from General Dwight D. Eisenhower.

A petite woman of 5 feet, 1 inch tall, Blanchfield was revered and referred to as "The Little Colonel" or "The Soldier's Nurse." She was a strong proponent of women serving and getting full recognition for service. Blanchfield hoped that the creation of a Regular Army Nurse Corps would encourage some of the women who served as nurses to pursue a career in the Army.

In her own words,

> Don't let anyone tell you that the combat zone is no place for nurses. It is, definitely. Just see what a bedside nurse can do to boost the morale of any injured Soldier. Just a pat on the head, blankets smoothed and a woman's smiling face for a man to look up into — sometimes it's better than plasma.[184]

---

183. Vane, 2014.
184. Ibid.

Reba Z. Whittle: The Forgotten POW

Born in Rocksprings, Texas, Reba Z. Whittle enlisted in the Army Nurse Corps in 1941 and was accepted by the Army Air Forces School of Air Evacuation to train as a flight nurse in 1943. Designed to help the nurses become largely self-sufficient during a flight, the course taught nurses like Whittle how to treat bleeding, pain, and shock without a physician.

In January 1944, Whittle departed for England, and between January and September 1944, she logged over 500 hours of flight time. On September 27, 1944, the day before she was supposed to go out with her boyfriend and see a USO show, Whittle left on a mission to collect casualties in Belgium.[185] The plane strayed into enemy territory and was shot down. Crashing about 2.5 miles outside Aachen, Whittle and the rest of the crew were captured by German soldiers and kept as prisoners of war. She kept a diary of her experiences until the end of November 1944.

First treated for their immediate injuries in a nearby German village, the crew was taken to the main Luftwaffe interrogation center, and Whittle was separated from the rest of the crew and lodged at a hospital. Through-out the month of October 1944, she was transferred several times to different POW hospitals where Whittle assisted in aiding wounded POWs.

Whittle was seen by representatives of the International Committee of the Red Cross, who in turn notified the State Department. Whittle would remain at a POW Stalag near Meiningen until she was repatriated, leaving the Stalag in January 1945.[186]

---

185. Yellin, 2004.
186. Frank, 1990.

Whittle received the Purple Heart on February 7, 1945 for the injuries she sustained during the plane crash and 10 days later received the Air Medal.[187] After the war, Whittle suffered from physical and psychiatric problems that seemed to be caused by her combat experience, but her many attempts for military medical retirement were mostly denied. For years, she was unknown as a POW. When Whittle died of cancer in 1981, many did not know of her experience as a POW.

In 1983, the Department of Defense and the Veterans Administration stated that it knew of no other American military women who had been taken prisoner besides the Army and Navy nurses captured and imprisoned by the Japanese. Whittle's widower Colonel Stanley Tobiason wrote to the Department of the Army, and on September 2, 1983, Whittle received official prisoner of war status posthumously.[188]

Whittle is unique in that she was the only nurse taken prisoner and the only American female military POW in the European Theater, although 68 Army nurses and 16 Navy nurses became POWs in the Pacific Theater.[189]

During World War II, 70,000 American women volunteered and served, risking their lives to serve the men fighting America's battles. Many of them served stateside, while others had the opportunity to serve overseas. Florence Blanchfield and Reba Whittle were just two of the women who supported the war effort through nursing.

Men who served in the military during World War II recommended their care and assistance years later, noting how much they appreciated seeing

---

187. Ibid.
188. Ibid.
189. Ibid.

a kind, feminine face when they were recovering from injuries. Although nursing had been somewhat available to women before the Second World War, female nurses became much more prevalent after the war because those 70,000 female nurses who served in World War II proved that nursing could be an appropriate occupation for a woman.

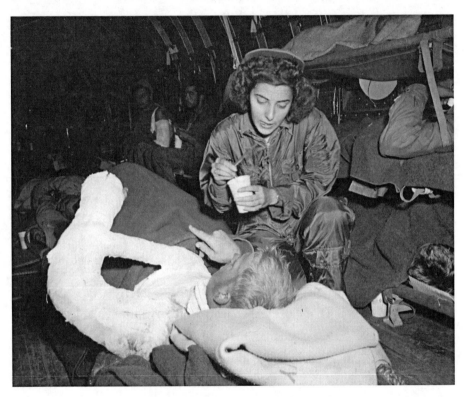

WWII flight nurse Jane Kendeigh

Chapter 8

"Wars Are Not Won by Respectable Methods"

Gaining information is always key to winning a war, and it was no different for World War II. Just as women had served as spies during World War I, including some who gained quite a reputation, women worked as spies during the Second World War. While it was perhaps a bit more acceptable than during World War I for females to participate in the war effort as spies, it still was frowned upon. Even so, some women were not afraid to become spies and were a great asset to their country's war effort.

In America, the Office of Strategic Services (OSS), the forerunner of the Central Intelligence Agency (CIA), oversaw information going in and out of enemy countries and within enemy military operations. Mainly focused overseas, the OSS aided resistance groups and sent information meant to sabotage the enemy in Axis-controlled areas.[190]

Of the 13,000 OSS employees who worked during the war, 4,000 of them were women, meaning that over 30 percent of the OSS workers were fe-

---

190. Yellin, 2004.

male.[191] Sometimes their job titles did not reflect what they actually did, as all women were told to say that they were file clerks.[192] For a choice few, this was false. They were actually spies.

Virginia Hall: "The Most Dangerous of All Allied Spies"

Reportedly considered by the Gestapo to be the most dangerous of all Allied spies, Virginia Hall was an expert spy and perhaps the most successful of World War II. She was an American spy who served with the British Special Operations Executive and later with the OSS. Hall had a variety of aliases, including "Camille," "Diane," "Germaine," "Marie of Lyon," "Marie Monin," and "Nicolas." And she successfully worked as a spy, even with a wooden leg!

Originally hoping to join the Foreign Service, Hall's hopes were dashed when she accidentally shot herself in the left leg while hunting in Izmir, Turkey. Her leg was amputated from the knee down, and she acquired a wooden leg, which she called "Cuthbert".

In the summer of 1940, Hall traveled from Vichy-controlled territory in France to London to volunteer for Britain's newly established Special Operations Executive (SOE). From August 1941 until November 1942, Hall coordinated resistance networks in France.

Even though the Germans were aware of her amputated leg from French double agents, calling her "the limping lady," Hall still remained undetected. She chose the disguise of an old rural woman who herded cattle and delivered goat's milk. Covering her legs with heavy skirts, the 38-year-old learned how to walk with a less detectable gait.[193]

---

191. Ibid.
192. Ibid.
193. Ibid.

When escaping the Nazis by traversing the Pyrenees mountains during the winter, Hall sent a message to the headquarters of SOE saying that she was fine, but "Cuthbert" was giving her trouble. Unaware that "Cuthbert" was the name of her wooden leg, the SOE replied with the message: "If Cuthbert is giving you difficulty, have him eliminated."[194]

When the Germans suddenly took over all of France in November 1942, Hall escaped to Spain and returned to England, where she was quietly awarded the Member of the British Empire medal for bravery. In 1944, Hall joined the U.S. OSS and returned to France as an old milkmaid or farmhand. She continued to provide information to London about German troop movements and assisted resistance groups, including one group of 30 resistance members with whom she worked quite closely.[195]

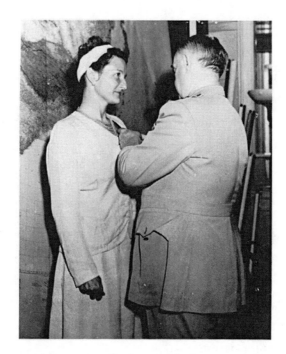

Virginia Hall receiving the distinguished service cross in 1945

---

194. "Virginia Hall," 2015.
195. Yellin, 2004.

Due to her valiant efforts, Hall received the Distinguished Service Cross, which was surpassed as the highest military award for bravery only by the Medal of Honor. She was the only American civilian woman who received this award during World War II. Hall would also go on to serve in the CIA from 1951 until 1965, supporting resistance groups in Iron Curtain countries.[196]

Amy Thorpe Pack: The Mata Hari of World War II

Born Amy Elizabeth Thorpe, Thorpe was known as "Betty" and traveled widely as a child due to her father's occupation as a U.S. Marine Corps officer. When Amy made her debut in Washington society at 18 years old, she drew men to her with her captivating green eyes and amber-colored hair.

She soon began an affair with Arthur Pack, a British embassy official who was 19 years her senior, which turned into a shaky marriage. Likely due to the fact that the Packs' first-born child — a son — was born five months after their wedding and thus clearly out of wedlock, Arthur asked his wife to give up their son for adoption. And they did. Even though they welcomed a daughter in 1934, Amy never seemed to forgive her husband, and they gradually grew apart.

Throughout the 1930s, Amy followed her husband to his various diplomatic postings in Europe and began to immerse herself in secret operations. She soon affiliated herself with both the British SOE and the American OSS, acquiring whatever information she could. Like French spy Mata Hari from World War I, who used her power to attract men and thus acquire information from them, Amy Thorpe Pack used her attractive looks to gather information.

---

196. "Virginia Hall," 2015.

In 1941, she formed a relationship with Charles Brousse, a Vichy press aide to the ambassador sympathetic to the Allies, in an attempt to gain access to the Vichy naval codes. In the midst of their affair, Pack and Brousse bribed night watchmen and security guards to successfully acquire the codes. Thanks to Pack's efforts to obtain these codes, she was credited for contributing to the success of the Allied invasion of North Africa.

When Germany invaded France in 1940, half of France came under Nazi control. The French government, which had been located in Paris, moved to Vichy, France, a city in the "Free Zone" unoccupied by the Nazis. While Paris was still technically the capital of France, Vichy was the de facto capital of France. Vichy France was named for the town in which the government resided, like the Weimar Republic in Germany.

Although Pack had achieved her objective, she and Brousse continued the affair, even letting Brousse's wife in on the secret that Pack was an Allied spy. Eager to support the Allied efforts, Mrs. Brousse even consented to introducing Pack, who was over 20 years younger than the Brousses, as their daughter. The three lived together in hotels, Mrs. Brousse completely unaware of the affair between her supposed daughter and her husband.

One day, however, Mrs. Brousse found out about the affair and threatened to reveal Pack's spy status. Even though Mrs. Brousse was sent to Mexico for so-called important clandestine work, Brousse and Pack's days of spying were over. Even so, Pack and Brousse remained an item and married after the war, living in a French château until Pack's death. Unfortunately, it did not turn out as well for their spouses: Arthur Pack committed suicide in 1945, and Brousse divorced his wife.

Pack is definitely a much more unconventional heroine. Her work in 1941 and 1942 saved countless American and British lives, but it came at the expense of her morals, although Pack reportedly wasn't ashamed:

My superiors told me that the results of my work saved thousands of British and American lives. Even one would have made it worthwhile. It involved me in situations from which 'respectable' women draw back — but mine was total commitment. Wars are not won by respectable methods.[197]

Julia McWilliams (later Julia Child): The Intelligence Officer Turned Cook

Much more well-known by her married name, Julia McWilliams (later Julia Child) joined the OSS in December 1942. She had wanted to join the WAVES or the WACs, but she was supposedly too tall at 6 feet, 2 inches.

While serving in the OSS, McWilliams had a variety of different jobs from serving as a junior research assistant to working as the head of the registry of records in the OSS office in Kandy, Ceylon (now Sri Lanka).

 FUN FACT McWilliams helped to develop shark repellent, which was an essential tool in winning the war. Curious sharks sometimes set off explosives intended for German-U boats when they bumped into said explosives. With the shark repellent, the explosives could take out their intended targets, not unsuspecting marine animals![198]

McWilliams never considered herself a spy, calling herself an office worker. Even so, her work as the head of the registry required a high security clearance, as she oversaw secret documents and sabotage reports. While it might not be accurate to call McWilliams a spy, she certainly was an intelligence officer, just not one undercover.

---

197. Yellin, 2004.
198. "A Look Back," 2007.

McWilliams was much more focused on the opportunity to live overseas in the Far East. In her words, "It just expanded my horizons… People all say that since World War II women have felt freer. I think they became a little more independent."[199] McWilliams took full advantage of her time in the Far East, even riding elephants.

During her time at Ceylon, McWilliams would meet her future husband, Paul Child, who was also an OSS Worker. Near the end of the war, they were both transferred to China, and it was there where McWilliams began her first forays into cooking. In fact, McWilliams believed that her interest in food first developed during her time as an OSS worker.

As McWilliams remembered, "American food in China was terrible; we thought it was cooked by grease monkeys. The Chinese food was wonderful, and we ate out as often as we could. That is when I became interested in food. I just loved Chinese food."[200]

Once the war ended, McWilliams and Child married. It was then that the Julia McWilliams that we know today — Julia Child — moved to Paris, went to the Cordon Bleu cooking school, and began her cooking career.

We may remember Julia Child more for cooking, but she still played an important role in the war effort as a quasi-spy, a woman with access to secret espionage material in a world before computers existed.

Spies are always the cool part of any war, but prior to World War II, they were almost exclusively men. While spying was still frowned upon for women in the 1940s, the work that Virginia Hall, Amy Thorpe Pack, Julia McWilliams (Child), and other women did for the OSS during the Second

---

199. Yellin, 2004.
200. Gaylord, 2012.

World War gave later women an in for the traditionally male-dominated positions. Whether it was assisted resistance groups in France, gaining information about the Vichy France naval codes, or working in an OSS office, the female spies are the relatively unknown, but highly significant heroes of World War II.

Chapter 9

Military (At Home and Overseas)

"You Are the Pioneers"

Depending on your nationality as a woman during World War II, you had different options available to you in the military. Some countries allowed women to join the military, but they could not serve overseas. Others had to participate in non-combat roles. Still others, like the Soviet Union, allowed women to serve in combat after 1941 in all military specialties, from cryptographer to antiaircraft gunner to scouts and even as sniper.

Overall, 450,000 to 500,000 women in America, 225,000 women in Britain, 500,000 women in Germany, and roughly one million women in the Soviet Union served in the military.[201]

In the United States, women could join an auxiliary unit like the Women's Army Auxiliary Corps (WAAC), named after the already established British WAAC, beginning in May 1942. Women who joined served under Oveta Culp Hobby, the first director of the WAAC. American women could also opt for the Women Airforce Service Pilots (WASP), created in August 1943 when the Women's Auxiliary Ferry Squadron (WAFS) and Women's Flying

---

201. Alexievich, 2017.

Training Detachment (WFTD) united, if they preferred to fly as test pilots and fly training planes.

Four WASPs at Lockbourne Air Force Base

American women could also join as official military members in other branches: the Navy's WAVES (Women Accepted for Volunteer Emergency Service), beginning in July 1942; the Coast Guard's SPAR (Semper Paratus, Always Ready), starting in November 1942; and finally, the Marines in February 1943. Women who joined the Marines were not given an official acronym — they were Marines. In September 1943, Congress granted the WAACs military status, removing the word "auxiliary" from their name. The WAAC became simply the Women's Army Corps (WAC).

 The difference between an auxiliary unit like the original WAAC (before September 1943) or WASP and the three other women's military branches (WAVES, SPAR, and female Marines) is that women who joined were civilians serving *with* the Army, while the WAVES, SPAR, and Marines were actually members of the military.

Unfortunately, as in the rest of the military at the time, the women's branches were racially segregated, if African Americans were allowed to joined at all. The WAC and Army Nurse Corps allowed for separate units composed of African American women. Near the end of the war, the WAVES and the SPAR opened up to black women, while black women were not admitted into the Marine Corps until after World War II. The WASP, which only lasted from August 5, 1943 until December 20, 1944, never allowed African American women.[202]

Unlike the other branches that did not permit women to serve overseas, WACs were allowed to go overseas, and the first WAAC battalion was sent overseas in early 1943.[203] By the end of the Second World War, WACS had served in every theater of operation, from North Africa to Europe to the Pacific.[204] Roughly 150,000 women eventually served in the WAAC/WAC during the war.

Although required to remain stateside — with the exception of the WAVES who were allowed to serve in American territories beginning in early 1945 — and often given boring clerical work, the 86,000 women who served in the WAVES, the roughly 11,000 women who joined the SPAR, the 1,100 women who served as WASPS, and the nearly 20,000 who joined the Marines were pioneers for women in the military.

---

202. Yellin, 2004.
203. Ibid.
204. Yellin, 2004.

As Captain Mary A. Hallaren, later director of the Women's Army Corps from 1947 to 1953, said to a group of WACs in England in 1945, "You are the pioneers. There were many bets against you when you first came . . . that you couldn't take it with the boys . . . Everyone who bet against you, lost."[205]

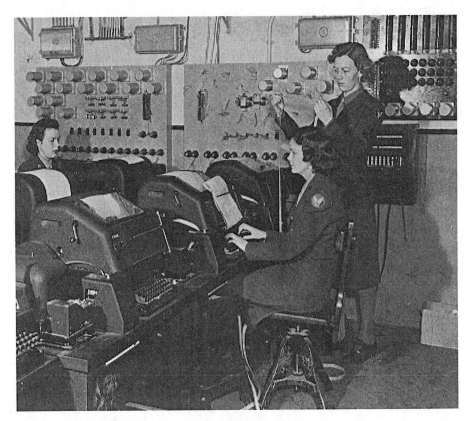

WAC teletype operators

Other countries boasted of strong female military members like Germany's Hanna Reitsch and Melitta von Stauffenberg, German aviatrixes and test pilots who flight-tested many of the Nazi's new aircraft. One of the only three women to receive the Iron Cross First Class, Reitsch was the first fe-

205. Ibid.

male helicopter pilot and one of the few pilots to fly the Focke-Achgelis Fa 61. She also flight tested the Me 262 and Me 163.

Another example are the roughly one million Soviet women who served, including the Russian Night Witches, female fighter pilots of World War II. The "Night Witches"— the German nickname for the 588th Night Bomber Regiment from 1942 to 1943 and the 46th Guards Night Bomber Aviation Regiment from 1943 to 1945 — was an all-female squadron of the Soviet Air Forces that was a deadly force and crucial to the Allied victory in World War II. The women flew a Polikarpov Po-2 and had the role of harassment and tactical bombing.

The 588th was the most highly decorated female unit in the Soviet Air Forces, as it flew over 30,000 missions during four years of the war and dropped a total of 23,000 tons of bombs on the invading Germans.[206] Its members ranged in age from 17 to 26.[207] They had no parachutes and no radar. As Nadezhda Popova, a commander of the squad who flew 852 missions herself, remembered, "Almost every time, we had to sail through a wall of enemy fire."[208]

Whether in America, Germany, the Soviet Union, or Britain, women were accomplishing amazing feats in the military.

Mary Churchill: The Prime Minister's Daughter Turned British WAAC

One's social status didn't have to impact one's service in the military, as Mary Churchill proved. Mary Spencer-Churchill was the youngest child

---

206. Garber, 2013.
207. Ibid.
208. Ibid.

born to Winston Churchill, the Prime Minister of Britain during most of the Second World War, and his wife Clementine.

Perhaps taking after her father, or even her mother, Mary could hold her own. From 1939 to 1941, she worked for the Red Cross and the Women's Voluntary Service. In 1941, Mary became one of the 190,000 women who would join the Auxiliary Territorial Service (ATS) — the British version of the WAAC. Among her contemporaries was the king's eldest daughter, Princess Elizabeth (now Queen Elizabeth II).

The prime minister was very proud of his daughter as she worked through the ranks of the ATS, which he mentioned in a letter to his son Randolph, speaking about the 230 women that Mary commanded as they set off for the front: "Not bad for 21!"[209]

Even so, Mary's father sometimes made it challenging for her during her military career. Sometimes, as she remembered, "I was received pretty frostily as everyone expected you to be above yourself. But once they discovered you scrubbed as many, if not more, floors as they did, they accepted one."[210] Mary's two longest postings were at Enfield and Hyde Park, conveniently located near her parents, but she was quite embarrassed by the geographical favorability of these postings.[211]

In 1946, just a couple months after her father had been replaced by Clement Attlee, Mary Churchill was demobilized from the ATS. Mary inspired not only countless Brits but also played a smart part in spurring Americans to adopt a WAAC program by gracing the ATS with her presence.

---

209. Soames, 2011.
210. Ibid.
211. Ibid.

Mary Amanda Sabourin: Pioneer for Women in the Marine Corps

Mary Amanda Sabourin, who first joined the Corps in 1945, was a pioneer for women Marines. Originally serving at the base's post exchange due to limited billets for females at the time, Sabourin was mobilized for the first time during the Korean War. She would become one of the first female Sergeant Majors in the Marine Corps.

Active in a variety of civic and military organizations, including serving as President of the Women Marines Association, Sabourin was proud to be a Marine and wasn't afraid to shut down any male Marines during World War II when they made fun of women joining.

As she later observed, "You're always going to find some people that . . . resent you. And some of the men resented [us] because we took their place and they had to go fight. . . . They would have their wise remarks."[212]

But those retorts didn't bother Sabourin. Whenever a male Marine referred to her as a BAM — or "Big-Ass Marine" — to her face, Sabourin would simply fire back, "And you're a HAM," the "H" standing for Half.[213] While some women may not have had the sass of Sabourin, they were willing to prove themselves as individuals qualified to serve in the military.

Whether women served in combat or in auxiliary roles, many countries saw a growing number of women serving in their militaries. Each country had its representative heroes: Hanna Reitsch and Melitta von Stauffenberg for Germany, the Night Witches for Soviet Russia, Mary Churchill for Great Britain, and women like Mary Amanda Sabourin (USMC) for the

---

212. Yellin, 2004.
213. Ibid.

United States. For American women, the pioneering contributions of the WACs and WASPs have remained an inspiration to this day. And rightly so, as they transformed the landscape of the United States military.

Chapter 10

Women Since World War II

"I Always Felt Like I'd Accomplished Something"

World War II completely changed the way that women were viewed. Before the Second World War, many women had one job and one job only: a stay-at-home mother who took charge of raising the children and keeping the house clean. When the absence of men required women to step up and serve in roles that they had never been in before, such as working in industrial factories or flying target boards for men to train on, women in America and all around the world rose to the occasion.

When the war ended in 1945, many women did go back to their former role as homemakers, as is evidenced by the phenomenon of the "Baby Boom." A lot of women, however, did not want to go back to the status quo. They really enjoyed the freedom that they had experienced and the opportunity to earn their own paycheck. As a 1944 U.S. Women's Bureau survey noted, 84 percent of women who worked in manufacturing wanted to keep their jobs in the factory.[214] As Lola Weixel noted, "I liked welding better. It was a special thing. At the end of the day I always felt I'd

---

214. Milkman, 1987.

accomplished something. It was good — there was a product, there was something to be seen."[215]

Some women did not try to fight their husbands to stay in the workforce. But others did and many others had supportive spouses. For those women, they sometimes worked and would come home and take care of the children in the evening — you start to see the rise of daycares after World War II — while others worked before having children but stayed at home after. Some women even left their husbands if they weren't supportive to their new career aspirations.

Even so, women still encountered significant opposition, often from men, when they desired to stay in the workforce. Their jobs, whether civilian or military, were seen as temporary, and many thought that if they stayed in the workforce, they would be taking positions away from men.

The women who chose to remain in the workforce following World War II are truly hidden in history. They endured hostility and resistance, yet still stayed in the workforce because they truly loved it. Modern working women owe the opportunities they have today to the pioneer women of the Second World War and the years immediately following.

In 1940, about a quarter of women worked outside of the home, largely in professions considered feminine, such as typing and sewing. Just a couple years after World War II, this number rose to almost a third of women working outside of the home.

The years after World War II also saw the rise of feminist groups like the Woman's Club of Winter Park where women gathered to promote an interest in the work of women. The feminist movement would not gain com-

---

215. Milkman, 1987Ibid.

plete traction until the 1960s and 1970s, but World War II had sown the seeds for it.

Finally, the WACs, WAVES, WASPs, SPAR, and women Marines led the way in full recognition of women in the military. In 1948, under President Harry Truman, the Women's Armed Services Integration Act was signed, recognizing women for the first time as full members of the American military, allowing them to claim the benefits of full members. Women now had the opportunity to serve in the military beyond times of war and could make a career in the Army or Navy.

On July 7, 1948, Secretary of the Navy John L. Sullivan swore in the first six enlisted women into the regular Navy.[216] About six months later, the Marine Corps followed suit, and five women in the New York City area were sworn into the Marine Corps on December 29, 1948 as the first "lady leathernecks" in the Metropolitan area.[217] The Army allowed hundreds of women to begin basic training before the end of the year.

In summary, the postwar years were a mixed bag for women. While they did experience some new opportunities like being able to serve as full permanent members in the military, the 1950s on the whole saw women going back to traditional roles as homemakers. It was not until the beginning of the second-wave feminism in the 1960s and 1970s that women's roles would change more conclusively and more permanently.

Betty Friedan: Identifier of "The Problem That Has No Name"

Born Bettye Naomi Goldstein in 1921, Friedan was active in both Marxist and Jewish circles. In 1938, she entered the all-female Smith College

---

216. "First Enlisted Women," 1948.
217. "5 Women Inducted Into the Marines," 1948.

as a freshman and graduated summa cum laude in 1942 with a major in psychology.

While she had spent a year at the University of California, Berkeley in 1943 and worked as a labor journalist in the 1940s and 1950s, Friedan's pinnacle work came in 1963. Encouraged in 1957 to conduct interviews of her class-mates for their 15th college reunion, Friedan focused on their education and their subsequent experiences in life as well as their current satisfaction in life.

At first, she began to publish articles discussing what she called "the prob-lem that has no name" and later decided to turn the articles into a book. Published in 1963, "The Feminine Mystique" described the widespread unhappiness of women as homemakers in the 1950s and early 1960s. Some women who wrote to Friedan said that they were glad to know that they were not alone.

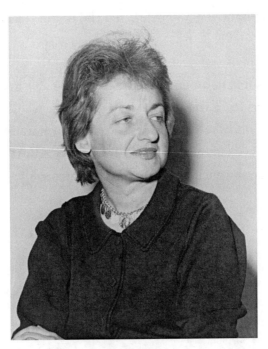

Betty Friedan

The 14-chapter book discussed the unfortunate effects of confining women into the domestic sphere, highlighting the lives of several homemakers across the United States. Friedan ended her book with an encouraging message to American women: she advised them to avoid being trapped in the feminine mystique by considering what it means to be feminine. As practical examples, Friedan even included examples of women who went against the feminine mystique and overcame it.

Somewhat surprisingly, "The Feminine Mystique" was extremely popular and became the bestselling nonfiction book in 1964 with over one million copies sold. Because Friedan had been willing to challenge the widely accepted belief that American women's true role in life was to be a wife and mother, her book opened the door for not only the feminist movement but also a widespread reconsideration of what it meant to be a woman in America.

"When All Those One Loved Best Were Gone"

For me, the most moving story was Vera Brittain's. You couldn't ask for an example of a more patriotic woman. She served as a British VAD nurse during much of the First World War, postponing a college career at Somerville College, Oxford — a significant accomplishment and an unusual desire for a woman in the 1910s — to take care of injured and dying men. She lost all of the men closest to her in the war, from her fiancé, Roland Leighton, to close friends Victor Richardson and Geoffrey Thurlow, to her brother Edward Brittain.

It was hard for Vera to start again "when all those one loved best were gone," in the words of Vera's daughter, Shirley Williams.[218] But life would continue as usual for Vera and countless women who had lost brothers, sons, and husbands in the war. Although originally caught up in the pomp and circumstance of marching off to war, Vera and other women in her generation soon realized the anguish and pain that it caused.

Williams reflected how the war had impacted Vera her entire life. Even though Vera was able to develop a friendship when she returned to college

---

218. Brittain, 2009.

with Winifred Holtby and later married George Catlin, a political scientist, in 1925, the war never left Vera completely. Her ashes were scattered on her brother's grave in Italy in 1970.

As Williams noted,

> My own picture of the War was gleaned from my mother. Her life, like that of so many of her contemporaries who were actually in the fighting or dealing with its consequences, was shaped by it and shadowed by it. It was hard for her to laugh unconstrainedly; at the back of her mind, the row upon row of wooden crosses were planted too deeply.[219]

Although I chose to end this book on a more somber note, I hope that you, as a much younger generation, have come to appreciate all that these incredible women did during World War I and World War II. I hope that you not only have been inspired and encouraged by their lives but also made aware of the anguish and pain that some of these women experienced. It is through the untold stories of not only triumph but also grief that you can have a full appreciation for the women of World War I and World War II.

---

219. Ibid.

I am a high school teacher, and in my free time, I enjoy reading about the 20th century, especially about World War II, and writing books. I have already written two books for Atlantic Publishing Group and had a wonderful experience working with Danielle Lieneman, my editor, so I was very excited to write another book.

I personally really enjoyed reading the oral histories of so many women who served in World War I and World War II. The almost 30,000 nurses who served overseas during World War II particularly captivated me in Monahan and Neidel-Greenlee's book "And If I Perish." Learning more about Vera Brittain and her famous book, "Testament of Youth," inspired me not only to watch the recent movie but also to read the entirety of her book. I also would highly recommend Liza Mundy's "Code Girls" about the American women codebreakers in World War II; it was so good that I finished it in just a couple days. To be honest, every primary and secondary source that I read had intriguing anecdotes, like a woman sniper who liked beautiful red scarfs and lost a sniper battle because of it and a woman who wore high heels into battle because she did not want to feel short. I always enjoyed when I read about women who had been teachers serving as nurses or military officers, like VAD nurse Olive Dent, as I appreciate finding similarities across generations and cultures.

Acknowledgements

Like any major project, I am indebted to several groups of people for their support and encouragement. As always, I am grateful to my students who will listen to stories from my reading and actively participate in class discussions, often asking questions that I am able to include in my book. In particular, I would like to thank my first class of freshmen who I had the opportunity to teach as seniors: Hannah Bono, Jake Dacier, Cole Duning, and Brendan Simpers. Your willingness to listen to me talk about history is a significant inspiration for me.

I am also very grateful for the staff at Atlantic Publishing Group. One could not ask for a better editor than Danielle. She is always helpful, encouraging, attentive, and thorough. Without Danielle, the process of writing a book would certainly be much less enjoyable.

Sair Wagner and the Petrina family have motivated me every step of the way, sometimes offering suggestions while other times simply being that uplifting voice. I deeply appreciate Gil Petrina getting me in touch with Mae Krier, an amazing woman who was one of the original Rosie the Riveters. I was so inspired by her story and felt fortunate to have had the opportunity to interview her. Finally, I am extremely grateful to my parents, Gary and LaRue Basinger and my sister and brother-in-law Rebekah and Daniel Slonim, for being as excited as I am about the book!

Alias: A false or assumed identify; often a pseudonym used by a spy

Aviatrix: A female pilot or aviator

Heir apparent: The person who is first in line to inherit the throne; no other person can inherit ahead of him or her

Night Witches: The bomber squadron of Soviet women who dropped 23,000 tons of bombs in German territory

Reparations: Generally known as the act of making amends for wrongs committee; in the context of war, it means the defeated country compensating the victors for war damages

Riveter: A person who takes a rivet, which is a metal bolt or pin with a head at one end, and hammers it with the rivet gun through pre-drilled holes in the body of an airplane; in essence, a riveter attaches sheets of metal together with thick metal pins

SPAR: The women's branch of the U.S. Coast Guard, which stands for Semper Paratus, Always Ready, and is based on the Coast Guard's Latin motto

Vigneron: A person who cultivates grapes for wine; a winegrower or winemaker

WAAC/WAC: Originally created as Women's Army Auxiliary Corps in 1942, it became known as the Women's Army Corps in 1943 when it was converted to active duty status in the Army

WASP: Women Airforce Service Pilots (WASP); created in August 1943 when the Women's Auxiliary Ferry Squadron (WAFS) and Women's Flying Training Detachment (WFTD) united

WAVES: The women's branch of the U.S. Navy created in July 1942 and known as Women Accepted for Volunteer Emergency Service to indicate that it was a temporary solution to appease older admirals who didn't want women in the military

Bibliography

"1914-1918: WWI – Women War Reports." *Hurry Up Sister Productions,* 2018, nojobforawoman.com/reporters/timeline/1914-1918-wwi/. Accessed 6 February 2018.

"5 Women Inducted Into the Marines; First 'Lady Leathernecks' in Metropolitan Area Take Oath as Regulars." *The New York Times,* 30 December, 1948, https://www.nytimes.com/1948/12/30/archives/5-women-inducted-into-the-marines-first-lady-leathernecks-in.html. Accessed 27 August 2018.

Alexievich, Svetlana. *The Unwomanly Face of War: An Oral History of Women in World War II.* Translated by Richard Pevear and Larissa Volokhonsky. Random House, 2017, p. 42.

Allcock, John B., and Antonia Young. *Black Lambs & Grey Falcons: Women Travellers in the Balkans.* Berghahn Books, 2000.

Atwood, Kathryn J. *Women Heroes of World War I: 16 Remarkable Resisters, Soldiers, Spies, and Medics.* Chicago Review Press, 2016.

Audoin-Rouzeau, Stéphane, and Annette Becker. *14-18: Understanding the Great War.* Translated by Catherine Temerson. Hill and Wang, 2002.

Beatty, Bessie. *The Red Heart of Russia*. The Century Company, 1918, p. 112.

Bochkareva, Maria, and Isaac Don Levine. *Yashka, My Life as Peasant, Officer and Exile*. Frederick A. Stokes Company, 1919.

Boissoneault, Lorraine. "The Women Who Fried Donuts and Dodged Bombs on the Front Lines of WWI." *Smithsonian Magazine*, 12 April 2017, www.smithsonianmag.com/history/donut-girls-wwi-helped-fill-soldiers-bellies-and-get-women-vote-180962864/. Accessed 16 November 2018.

Bourke, Joanna. "Women and the Military During World War One." *BBC News*, 3 March 2011, www.bbc.co.uk/history/british/britain_wwone/women_combatants_01.shtml. Accessed 12 June 2018.

Brittain, Vera. *Testament of Youth*. Orion Publishing Group, 2009.

Brocklehurst, Steven. "The female war medic who refused to 'go home and sit still.'" *BBC News*, 26 November 2017, www.bbc.com/news/uk-scotland-42096350. Accessed 19 February 2018.

Chisholm, Hugh, ed. "Cavell, Edith." *Encyclopædia Britannica*. 12th ed., London & New York, 1922.

Craydon, Barbara. "The Love Tricks of the Woman Spy." *The Daily Ardmoreite* (Ardmore, Oklahoma), 13 February 1918. *Chronicling America: Historic American Newspapers*. Lib. of Congress. chroniclingamerica.loc.gov/lccn/sn85042303/1918-02-13/ed-1/seq-6/. Accessed 30 January 2018.

Crocker, Betty. *Your Share: How to Prepare Appetizing, Healthful Meals with Foods Available Today*. General Mills, Incorporated, 1943.

Day, Elizabeth. "*Testament of Youth*: Vera Brittain's classic, 80 years on." *The Guardian*, 23 March 2013, www.theguardian.com/books/2013/mar/24/vera-brittain-testament-of-youth. Accessed 14 February 2018.

"D-Day Landings: Operation Overlord in Numbers." *The Telegraph*, 6 June 2016, www.telegraph.co.uk/news/2016/06/06/d-day-landings-operation-overlord-in-numbers2/the-allied-casualties-figures-for-d-day-have-generally-been-esti/. Accessed 14 June 2018.

Dent, Olive. *A Volunteer Nurse on the Western Front: Memoirs from a WWI Camp Hospital*. Random House, 2014.

Doty, Madeleine Zabriskie. *Short Rations: An American Woman in Germany, 1915-1916*. Century Company, 1917.

Dunbar, Ruth. "Chivalrous Men Would Stay the Law's Hand While Women Deny Their Own Right to Privileges." *New-York Tribune*, 31 October 1915. *Chronicling America: Historic American Newspapers*. Lib. of Congress. chroniclingamerica.loc.gov/lccn/sn83030214/1915-10-31/ed-1/seq-33/. Accessed 30 January 2018.

"Elsie Inglis to be commemorated for war achievements." *BBC News*, 8 November 2017, www.bbc.com/news/uk-scotland-edinburgh-east-fife-41915396. Accessed 19 February 2018.

"First Enlisted Women Are Sworn In by Navy; Sullivan Hails Event as Service Milestone." *The New York Times*, 8 July 1948, https://www.nytimes.com/1948/07/08/archives/first-enlisted-women-are-sworn-in-by-navy-sullivan-hails-event-as.html. Accessed 27 August 2018.

Frank, Mary E.V. "The Forgotten POW: Second Lieutenant Reba Z. Whittle." *Defense Technical Information Center*, 1 February 1990, www.dtic.mil/dtic/tr/fulltext/u2/a223404.pdf. Accessed 30 July 2018.

Garber, Megan. "Night Witches: The Female Fighter Pilots of World War II." *The Atlantic*, 15 July 2013, www.theatlantic.com/technology/archive/2013/07/night-witches-the-female-fighter-pilots-of-world-war-ii/277779/. Accessed 30 July 2018.

Gavin, Lettie. *American Women in World War I: They Also Served.* University Press of Colorado, 2006, pp. 4, 26.

Gaylord, Chris. "Julia Child was a spy. Was she any good at it?" *The Christian Science Monitor*, 15 August 2012, www.csmonitor.com/Technology/Tech-Culture/2012/0815/Julia-Child-was-a-spy.-Was-she-any-good-at-it. Accessed 30 July 2018.

Graves, Donna. "Tending the Homefront: The Many Roles of Bay Area Women During World War II." *National Park Service*, www.nps.gov/nr/travel/wwiibayarea/womenatwar.htm. Accessed 29 July 2018.

"The Great War — Casualties and Deaths." *Public Broadcasting Service*, www.pbs.org/greatwar/resources/casdeath_pop.html. Accessed 15 June 2017.

Hall, Mitchell K, editor. *Opposition to War: An Encyclopedia of U.S. Peace and Antiwar Movements.* ABC-CLIO, 2018, p. 213-14.

Harris, Carolyn. "The Women Warriors of the Russian Revolution." *Smithsonian*, 28 April 2017, www.smithsonianmag.com/history/women-warriors-russian-revolution-180963067/. Accessed 19 March 2018.

Hartley, Cathy, editor. "Inglis, Elsie Maud." *A Historical Dictionary of British Women.* Psychology Press, 2003, p. 237.

Hoehling, A.A. *Women Who Spied.* Madison Books, 1992, p. 69.

Jankowski, Paul. *Verdun: The Longest Battle in the War.* Oxford University Press, 2014.

Johnson, Paul. *Churchill*. Viking, 2009.

King, Henry Churchill. *Fundamental Questions*. Macmillan, 1917, p. 241.

Kladstrup, Don, and Petie Kladstrup. *Champagne: How the World's Most Glamorous Wine Triumphed Over War and Hard Times*. Harper Perennial, 2006.

Knox, Alfred. *With the Russian Army 1914-1917: Being Chiefly Extracts from the Diary of a Military Attaché*, Volume II. Hutchinson & Co., 1921, p. 711.

Lawrence, Dorothy. *Sapper Dorothy Lawrence: The Only English Woman Soldier, Late Royal Engineers, 51st Division, 179th Tunnelling Company, B. E. F.* J. Lane, 1919.

Lebergott, Stanley. "Labor Force and Employment, 1800-1960." *Output, Employment, and Productivity in the United States after 1800*, edited by Dorothy S. Brady, National Bureau of Economic Research, 1966, pp. 117-204.

Litoff, Judy Barrett, and David C. Smith. "To the Rescue of the Crops." *Prologue* vol. 25, no. 4, Winter 1993, www.archives.gov/publications/prologue/1993/winter/landarmy.html. Accessed 29 July 2018.

"A Look Back . . . Julia Child: Life Before French Cuisine." *Central Intelligence Agency*, 13 December 2007, www.cia.gov/news-information/featured-story-archive/2007-featured-story-archive/julia-child.html. Accessed 30 July 2018.

Lukacs, John. *The Legacy of the Second World War*. Yale University Press, 2010, p. 8.

MacLeod, Charlotte. *Had She But Known: A Biography of Mary Roberts Rinehart*. Open Road Media, 2016.

Manning, Molly Guptil. *When Books Went to War: The Stories That Helped Us Win World War II*. Houghton Mifflin Harcourt, 2014, p. 11.

Marzouk, Lawrence. "Girl Who Fought Like a Man." *Times*, 20 November 2003, www.times-series.co.uk/nostalgia/432132.Girl_who_fought_like_a_man/. Accessed 8 February 2018.

Mason, Amanda. "What was the Women's Land Army?" *The Imperial War Museum*, 30 January 2018, www.iwm.org.uk/history/what-was-the-womens-land-army. Accessed 29 July 2018.

McKenna, Marthe. *I Was a Spy: The Classic Account of Behind-the-Lines Espionage in the First World War*. Pool of London Press, 2015.

Milkman, Ruth. *Gender at Work; The Dynamics of Job Segregation by Sex During World War II*. University of Illinois Press, 1987.

Miller, Louise. *A Fine Brother: The Life of Captain Flora Sandes*. Alma Books, 2012.

Mintz, S., and S. McNeil. "World War II Guide: Wartime Hollywood." *Digital History*, 2018, www.digitalhistory.uh.edu/teachers/modules/ww2/wartimehollywood.html. Accessed 30 July 2018.

Montgelas, Max, and Walther Schücking, editors. *Outbreak of the World War: German Documents Collected by Karl Kautsky*. Oxford University Press, 1924, pp. 78-79.

Mundy, Liza. *Code Girls: The Untold Story of the American Women Code Breakers of World War II*. Hachette Books, 2017.

"The Paris Peace Conference and the Treaty of Versailles." *Office of the Historian*, history.state.gov/milestones/1914-1920/paris-peace. Accessed 21 July 2017.

Noonan, Norma C., and Carol Nechemias, editors. *Encyclopedia of Russian Women's Movements*. Greenwood Publishing Group, 2001, p. 105.

Pasvolsky, Leo. "The Heroines of Free Russia." *The Red Cross Magazine*, February 1918, pp. 11-15.

Pierce, John R. "Florence A. Blanchfield: A Lifetime of Nursing Leadership." *Federal Practitioner*, September 2017, www.mdedge.com/sites/default/files/Document/September-2017/0917fed_history.pdf. Accessed 30 July 2018.

Powell, Anne. *Women in the War Zone*. The History Press, 2016.

Quigley, Samantha L. "Thanks for the Memories: Judy Garland." *USO*, 13 December 2015, www.uso.org/stories/120-thanks-for-the-memories-judy-garland. Accessed 30 July 2018.

Rinehart, Mary Roberts. *The Altar of Freedom*. Houghton Mifflin, 1917.

———. *Kings, Queens and Pawns: An American Woman on the Front*. George H. Doran Company, 1915.

Rose, Kenneth David. *Myth and the Greatest Generation: A Social History of Americans in World War II*. Routledge, 2008, p. 177.

"Rosie the Riveter." *History.com*, 2010, www.history.com/topics/world-war-ii/rosie-the-riveter. Accessed 29 July 2018.

Sandes, Flora. *The Autobiography of a Woman Soldier: A Brief Record of Adventure with the Serbian Army, 1916-1919*. H. F. & G. Witherby, 1927, p. 220.

Soames, Emma. "Mary Churchill: The Secret Life of Winston Churchill's Daughter." *The Telegraph*, 3 October 2011, www.telegraph.co.uk/culture/books/8858648/Mary-Churchill-the-secret-life-of-Winston-Churchills-daughter.html. Accessed 30 July 2018.

Sorrel, Nancy Caldwell. *The Women Who Wrote the War: The Compelling Story of the Path-breaking Women War Correspondents of World War II*. Skyhorse Publishing Inc., 2011.

Stroe, Ilinca. "1917: Romania's First Female Second Lieutenant." *Study Romanian,* 9 November 2017, www.studyromanian.com/single-post/ Romanias-First-Female-Second-Lieutenant. Accessed 12 June 2018.

Suddaby, Steve. "Attempts to Kill the Kaiser From the Air." *The '14-'18 Journal,* 2007, pp. 44-46, www.ww1aero.org.au/pdfs/Sample%20 Journal%20Articles/kaiser%202007.pdf. Accessed 5 February 2018.

Suddath, Claire. "Why Did World War I Just End?" *Time,* 4 October 2010, content.time.com/time/world/article/0,8599,2023140,00. html. Accessed 29 July 2017.

Vane, Betsy. "Blanchfield, 'The Soldier's Nurse,' Paved Way as Army Pioneer." *The Fort Campbell Courier,* 27 March 2014, fortcampbellcourier.com/news/article_fa855882-b5fa-11e3-b8e7-0019bb2963f4.html. Accessed 30 July 2018.

"Virginia Hall: The Courage and Daring of 'The Limping Lady.'" *Central Intelligence Agency,* 8 October 2015, www.cia.gov/news-information/featured-story-archive/2015-featured-story-archive/ virginia-hall-the-courage-and-daring-of-the-limping-lady.html. Accessed 30 July 2018.

"V-Mail." Smithsonian *National Postal Museum,* postalmuseum.si.edu/ exhibits/past/the-art-of-cards-and-letters/mail-call/v-mail.html. Accessed 29 July 2018.

"War Production." *PBS,* September 2007, www.pbs.org/thewar/at_ home_war_production.htm. Accessed 29 July 2018.

West, Rebecca. "Extraordinary Exile." *The New Yorker,* 7 September 1946, www.newyorker.com/magazine/1946/09/07/extraordinary-exile. Accessed 30 July 2018.

Wilson, Woodrow. "Fourteen Points." Yale Law School Lillian Goldman Law Library, 8 January 1918, avalon.law.yale.edu/20th_century/wilson14.asp. Accessed 29 July 2017.

Yellin, Emily. *Our Mothers' War: American Women at Home and at the Front During World War II.* Free Press, 2004.

Rachel Basinger taught history and other humanities classes to ninth and 12th graders at a small private school in Williamsburg, Virginia for the past four years and started her fifth year of teaching at another small private school in Jacksonville, North Carolina, again teaching history and other humanities classes to middle schoolers and high schoolers.

She received a bachelor's degree in history and Spanish from Hillsdale College in 2014. Many of the elective classes she took focused on modern history, and she wrote two undergraduate theses on Spanish anarchism and national identity in Spain and France. A history buff, she loves to study 19th- and 20th-century history, especially the World Wars and the Cold War. She has written two other books for Atlantic Publishing Group: "Events That Changed the Course of History: The Story of the World War I Armistice 100 Years Later" and "People That Changed the Course of History: The Story of Karl Marx 200 Years After His Birth".